KV-622-941

£2.50

WONDERS OF MAN

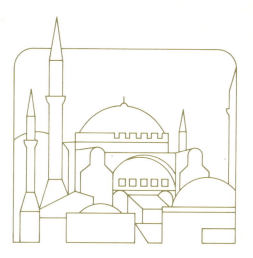

Jill Murray.

HAGIA SOPHIA

by Lord Kinross

and the Editors
of the Newsweek Book Division

Published in the United Kingdom by

The Reader's Digest Association Limited, London

in association with

NEWSWEEK, New York

NEWSWEEK BOOK DIVISION

JOSEPH L. GARDNER   *Editor*

Janet Czarnetzki   *Art Director*

Edwin D. Bayrd, Jr.   *Associate Editor*

Laurie P. Phillips   *Picture Editor*

Eva Galan   *Assistant Editor*

Lynne H. Brown   *Copy Editor*

Russell Ash   *European Correspondent*

ALVIN GARFIN   *Publisher*

WONDERS OF MAN

MILTON GENDEL   *Consulting Editor*

© READER'S DIGEST is a registered trademark of The Reader's
Digest Association Inc., of Pleasantville, New York, U.S.A.
Published by

THE READER'S DIGEST ASSOCIATION LIMITED
25 Berkeley Square London W1X 6AB

London New York Montreal Sydney Cape Town

© 1973 — Arnoldo Mondadori Editore, S.p.A.
All rights reserved. Printed and bound in Italy.

Contents

A tenth-century chalice, decorated with
semiprecious stones and enameled plaques

Title page:
A twelfth-century incense burner that suggests in
miniature the shape of the Church of Hagia Sophia

Introduction

The cavernous interior of Hagia Sophia reflects more than fourteen centuries of continuous use — first as a Christian church, then as a Moslem mosque, and finally as a secular museum. The decor (left) is an amalgam of styles — the result of successive restorations that began when the original, fourth-century structure was completely gutted by fire in A.D. 532. Entirely rebuilt and extravagantly redecorated by Emperor Justinian the Great, Hagia Sophia reopened its massive bronze doors a mere five years later. Gold mosaic-work covered the dome and the vaults, and rare marbles from Thessaly, Egypt, and Lydia gleamed in the galleries. In time, both the great dome and its flanking arches were embellished with mesmerizing figural mosaics.

Following the conquest of Constantinople in 1453, the Ottoman Turks stripped Hagia Sophia of its Christian ornaments, installed a raised sultan's box (center) in place of the pulpit, and affixed huge circular disks emblazoned with Koranic verses to the pediments. The figural mosaics were obliterated with whitewash — in response to the Moslem prohibition of any representation of the human form — and it was not until the mid-nineteenth century, as the Ottoman Empire sank into its final decline, that a serious attempt was at last made to restore the building's neglected interior to its original splendor. That painstaking effort was resumed in 1932 when the Byzantine Institute of America obtained permission to begin the tedious process of uncovering the fragmentary remains of Hagia Sophia's once-luminous mosaics. Through diligence and devotion, the glories of Justinian's church are being reclaimed from the grime that dims their luster.

THE EDITORS

Men of Constantinople praying in Hagia Sophia, from a thirteenth-century miniature.

HAGIA SOPHIA
IN HISTORY

I
The New Rome

As the Roman Empire declined and fell, a new empire was born — the Byzantine. Its birth was a turning point in history; its life was to span eleven hundred years. Rooted in the classical traditions of Greece and Rome, the Byzantine Greeks rejected the dying pagan gods of those cultures and evolved a living Christian civilization. Their capital was the New Rome, Constantinople; their sacred shrine, succeeding the temple of the Pantheon, was the Church of Hagia Sophia, the Holy Wisdom, consecrated to the one God alone. This great church rose in the sixth century — a symbol of Christ's wisdom; a masterpiece of volume, scale, and architectural style; an embodiment of the power, grandeur, and spirit of a mighty empire, uniting East with West.

Hagia Sophia appears today much as the Byzantine historian Procopius described it more than fourteen centuries ago:

[A] spectacle of marvellous beauty, overwhelming to those who see it, but to those who know it by hearsay altogether incredible. For it soars to a height to match the sky, and as if surging up from the other buildings it stands on high and looks down on the remainder of the city. . . . Both its breadth and its length have been so carefully proportioned, that it may not improperly be said to be exceedingly long and at the same time unusually broad. And it exults in an indescribable beauty. For it proudly reveals its mass and the harmony of its proportions, having neither any excess nor deficiency, since it is both more pretentious than the buildings to which we are accustomed, and considerably more noble than those which are merely huge, and it bounds exceedingly in sunlight and in the reflection of the sun's rays from the marble.

Noting that the interior of the great church seemed to be illuminated not only from without but by a radiance from within, Procopius declared: ". . . whenever anyone enters this church to pray, he understands at once that it is not by any human power or skill, but by the influence of God, that this work has been so finely turned."

The interior is described in equally lyrical terms by a contemporary Byzantine poet, Paul the Silentiary:

Whoever raises his eyes to the beauteous firmament of the roof, scarce dares to gaze on its rounded expanse sprinkled with the stars of heaven, but turns to the fresh green marble below, seeming as it were to see the flower-bordered streams of Thessaly, and budding corn, and woods thick with trees; leaping flocks too and twining olive-trees, and the vine with green tendrils, or the deep blue peace of summer sea, broken by the plashing oars of sea-girt ship. Whoever puts foot within the sacred fane, would live there, for ever, and his eyes well with tears of joy.

To Michael of Thessalonica, a twelfth-century scribe, the church was a "tent of the heavens, which man indeed has set up, although God has surely taken part in the work." Within its triple doors, symbolizing the Holy Trinity, "the building lies open forming an immense space, having a hollowness so capacious that it might be pregnant with many thousands of bodies and a height so great as to turn the head, and make the eyes stop still as it were at the zenith."

According to this Greek chronicler, the gilded roof of the church flashed in the sunlight with such brilliance that the gold seemed to flow from the dome in a molten stream. Precious metals had also been lavished

The intricate Byzantine ivories that appear at the opening of this and the succeeding chapters depict imperial, mythological, and religious themes.

on the interior of the church. The Holy Table, or altar, was of gold. Silver too abounded — 40,000 pounds of it in the sanctuary alone. The screen and the canopy above the altar were of silver, and the stalls of the priests were plated with silver. Thus enriched, the church was dedicated by the Emperor Justinian on December 27, 537.

That was a ceremony to be repeated each year on the same date for nine centuries to come. The emperor led the way into the great church, where, in the words of an anonymous recorder, "the first gleam of light rosy-armed driving away the great shadows leapt from arch to arch" and "all the princes and people with one voice hymned their songs of prayer and praise." Hand in hand with the patriarch, Justinian proceeded down the nave, prostrated himself before the altar, and entered the sanctuary. There he kissed the holy chalices, the golden patens, the corporal cloth, and the holy gilded cross — and there he played his role in the sacred drama of the Divine Liturgy.

On the day of this historic inauguration Justinian emerged in state from his palace in a four-horse chariot. He sacrificed 1,000 oxen, 6,000 sheep, 600 stags, and some 10,000 birds before giving 30,000 bushels of meal to the poor and needy. Accompanied by the patriarch, he then proceeded to the church. Entering its royal gates, the emperor released the patriarch's hand, which he had been holding, and hastened on alone into the ambo. Extending his arms toward heaven, he cried, "Glory to God, Who has deemed me worthy of fulfilling such a work. O Solomon, I have surpassed thee."

Justinian's proud declaration was approved by many contemporaries. Paul the Silentiary compared the church to a pharos, a spiritual lighthouse: "The sacred light cheers all: even the sailor guiding his bark on the waves, leaving behind him the unfriendly billows of the raging Pontus, and winding a sinuous course amidst creeks and rocks . . . does not guide his laden vessel by the light of Cynosure, or the circling bear, but by the divine light of the church itself."

The sea, Procopius notes, "surrounds Constantinople like a garland." From the site of its former acropolis, the great domed monument of Hagia Sophia commands the waves. Set on a jutting triangular headland that has long been a focal point of world geography, the city confronts the confluence of two seas, north and south, and the meeting of two continents, east and west (see map, page 17). Through the narrow, swift-flowing straits of the Bosporus (in English the "Ox Ford"), the waters flow south from the Black Sea (the classical Euxine washing the Pontic shores) into the Sea of Marmara (the classical Propontis), and then out through the strait of the Dardanelles into the Aegean and Mediterranean seas beyond. Between the Bosporus and the Sea of Marmara there curves inland a long, narrow natural harbor known as the Golden Horn. Shaped like the horn of an ox or stag, it became golden, as Gibbon expresses it, "from the riches which every wind wafted from the most distant countries into the secure and capacious port of Constantinople."

The ancient Greeks were the first people to develop these trade routes. Following Jason and his Argonauts, who sailed up the Bosporus into the Black Sea to seek the Golden Fleece — and following Agamemnon and his Achaeans, who fought the Trojans for control of the Hellespont — there came, in the course of recorded

history, groups of seafaring colonists from the Greek seaport of Megara. The first of them settled on the Asian shore of the Bosporus, founding a colony at Chalcedon. Legend relates that the second, preparing to set forth around 658 B.C. under a leader named Byzas, first consulted the oracle at Delphi on the choice of a site. Byzas was advised to settle "opposite to the land of the blind men." Correctly interpreting this cryptic phrase, he founded his colony on the European shore, across the Bosporus from Chalcedon. In their blindness, the earlier colonists had established their settlement on a bay beset by winds, ignorant of the superior advantages of the secure harbor opposite, "made by nature never to be stormy." There the city of Byzantium was built.

Thus, from the first, geography conditioned Byzantium's history. The colony founded by Byzas evolved from a Greek trading settlement into the vital eastern nexus of the Roman Empire. At the end of the second century A.D. the city was extensively rebuilt by Septimius Severus. In the following century Diocletian divided the empire into two and ruled over its eastern part from Nicomedia, a port at the head of a gulf on the Asian shore of the Sea of Marmara. Constantine the Great, who had served under Diocletian as a youth, reunited the two parts in A.D. 324, but decided to rule over both from a new eastern capital. Rejecting Nicomedia and toying only briefly — and perhaps apocryphally — with the notion of founding his capital on the site of ancient Troy, Constantine soon settled on Byzantium — whose strategic advantages he was quick to perceive. According to legend, he was encouraged by a flock of eagles that descended upon a prospective

site near Chalcedon, seized the emperor's stores and measuring-tapes in their claws, and flew with them across the Bosporus to the city of Byzas.

In his choice of the East as the new center of imperial power, Constantine was influenced, among other factors, by his attitude toward the Christian religion. A dynastic representative on earth of the divine Hercules, he was still worshiping the pagan gods of his ancestors as he neared the age of forty. The emperor was devoted also to the sun-god Apollo, whose cult prevailed among the Oriental followers of Zoroaster and Mithras. But a new religious cult, that of the Christians, was slowly gaining ground in the empire, particularly in the East, where the early Christian Fathers had first effectively spread the Gospel. This development had led, under Diocletian, to a policy of persecution that had ended in failure. Constantine, on the other hand, was a tolerant monotheist who realized that the empire, in its decadence, needed not merely a strong governmental structure but a new spiritual force to replace polytheism. And since his capture of Rome in A.D. 312, he had been moving slowly toward the acceptance of new religious ideas.

The battle of the Milvian Bridge, which had led to the routing of Constantine's rival, Maxentius, and to the conquest of Rome, was traditionally said to have been fought and won beneath the rays not of the divine sun-god but of a cross in the heavens. Seen athwart the sun by the invading troops on the eve of battle, that cross had borne the legend *"In Hoc Signo Vinces"* — "By this sign thou shalt conquer." Tradition asserts that this miraculous vision was confirmed that night by a dream in which the emperor was bidden by Christ

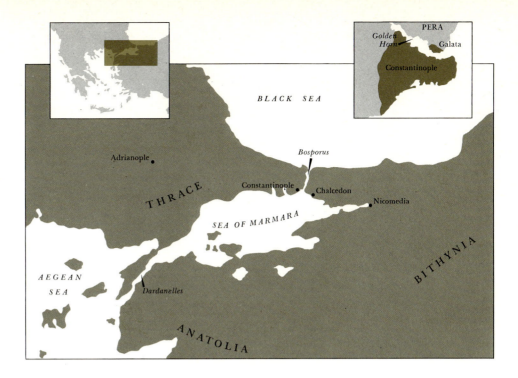

The battle of the Milvian Bridge (left), in which Constantine the Great routed his rival Maxentius, was to have major ecclesiastical and political repercussions. Fourteen years later, in A.D. 326, the victorious emperor laid out the boundaries of the city that was to bear his name for more than a millennium. Situated at the east end of the Sea of Marmara (right), the new capital of Constantinople surveyed both the Bosporus and the Golden Horn (see map inset at the upper right).

to adopt the sign. When he awoke, Constantine ordered that the sign of the cross be inscribed on the shields of his soldiery in the form of a Christian monogram, a cross with a loop on top of it. The emperor's subsequent campaigns were likewise waged under this sign, stamped on the banners and shields of his army and embodied in the *labarum,* a standard in the form of a pike with a cross-piece surmounted by a crown and incorporating a similar monogram.

Henceforth, observes Gibbon, "The piety of Constantine was admitted as an unexceptionable proof of the justice of his arms; and his use of victory confirmed the opinion of the Christians that their hero was inspired, and conducted, by the Lord of Hosts." So Constantine's soldiers marched to battle with the full assurance that the same God who had opened a passage through the Red Sea and had buckled the walls of Jericho at the sound of the trumpets of Joshua would display His power by securing victories for Rome's pious monarch.

In 313, a few months after his conquest of Rome, Constantine issued the Edict of Milan, which reversed the former edicts of persecution. It granted free religious and civil rights to the Christian communities, restoring to the Christian Church its places of assembly and worship and its confiscated property, with indemnification from the imperial treasury to any who had purchased such property. Toleration of Christianity was thus officially and generally established. Constantine became revered as the equal of the Apostles and the vice-regent of Christ on earth. Blending the temporal powers of Caesar with the spiritual authority of the Church, he ruled supreme over both Church and State,

an absolute Oriental monarch with semidivine status.

Constantine's new capital was a city inspired not by the Delphic oracle but by the Christian God. The emperor laid it out in person — with divine assistance. According to legend, he strode across the site, tracing Byzantium's boundaries with the tip of his lance. As he continued to walk, he exceeded the bounds of the existing city. Asked by an anxious assistant where he intended to stop, Constantine replied, "I shall still advance, till He, the invisible guide who marches before me, thinks proper to stop." The city thus demarcated was four times the size of its Roman predecessor; lying between the Golden Horn and the Sea of Marmara, it was fortified by new land walls and additional seawalls.

Constantinople, as the new metropolis came to be known, aspired to be a new Rome. Like the old Rome, it was built upon a cluster of hills — initially five, but later extended to seven. Classical in aspect and character, it embodied many traditional features of ancient Rome: a capitol, an octagon, extensive public baths, an imperial palace, and a building for the senate — a body unlikely, under so autocratic a regime, to have served more than a formal purpose. Constantine built his forum on the second hill. Its oval, marble-paved area had a porphyry column in the center that towered more than a hundred feet high. The column in turn was surmounted by a colossal bronze statue of Constantine as Apollo the sun-god, with a scepter in one hand and a globe in the other. The rays from his crown, shining down on the city, were said to incorporate nails from the True Cross.

Enclosed in the marble pedestal of the column, so

The noble visage at right is believed to be a bronze portrayal of Constantine — whose martial temperament was counterbalanced by the piety of his mother, Helena. Posed behind a pair of imperial eagles in the luminous cameo at left are Helena, her son, her daughter-in-law Fausta, and her grandsons Constantius II and Crispus.

legend relates, were trophies of both the pagan and the Christian traditions. Here was the Palladium, the wooden image of the protective goddess Pallas Athene, retrieved from Troy by Aeneas and later purloined from Rome. Here were relics of both Old and New Testament origin: the adze with which Noah built the ark; a piece of the rock that Moses struck with his rod to produce water; crumbs from the loaves of Christ's miracle at Cana in Galilee; fragments of the crosses from Calvary; the alabaster box of spikenard ointment from which Christ's feet were anointed; and relics of several saints. Constantine's column — which still survives in a charred, truncated form — thus served as an appropriate cult object for pagan, Mithraist, and Christian alike.

In final emulation of Rome the emperor completed, embellished, and enlarged the Hippodrome built by Septimius Severus. The grandiose arena was intended to serve as the secular axis of the Byzantine world. Disposed along the spina, the low central partition of the race track that led toward the imperial box, were a laurel-wreathed bust of the emperor, statues from Greece, and the bronze Serpentine Column from Delphi. (The last had been erected as a tribute to the Delphic oracle in celebration of the Greeks' victory over the Persians at the battle of Plataea.) Elsewhere in the new capital were sculptures collected from all parts of the Greco-Roman world. As Saint Jerome was to write: "Constantinople is dedicated while nearly every other city is stripped bare."

Constantine's change of religious belief evolved gradually toward a synthesis of Greco-Roman and Oriental philosophy. As that synthesis took place, the em-

peror's political acumen led him to steer a middle course between his pagan and Christian subjects. Pagan worship continued side by side with Christian; old temples continued to stand, and two new ones were built for the use of the pagan labor force employed on the city's construction. One, near the Hippodrome, was dedicated to Castor and Pollux; the other was dedicated to Tyche, the tutelary goddess who traditionally brought fortune to the city and hence was portrayed with a cornucopia in her hand. (Later she was also depicted with a cross on her forehead.)

During this same period Constantine built a number of churches. In these he departed entirely from the architectural style of the pagan temple, evolving instead a new form of the Roman secular building, the basilica — a not inappropriate choice since Church was now equated with State. The Roman basilica, which took various forms, was in essence a large meeting hall designed to serve as a market, a stock exchange, a court of law, the drill hall of a barracks, or the audience hall of a palace. Oblong in shape, it generally had a central pillared aisle, lit by a clerestory, that led to an apse and a raised dais. There, on a rounded tier of seats, the emperor, magistrate, or presiding official and his attendants would sit.

To adapt the design of such a building for the purpose of Christian worship, to make of it an assembly hall for the Apostolic and Catholic congregation, was simple enough, involving no more than the conversion of the dais into a bishop's throne, with seats for his clergy around it and an altar in front. A narthex, or vestibule, was added to the entrance so that unbaptized converts could listen to the service, and a baptistery was

The wealthy aristocratic families who settled in Constantine's new Eastern capital could enjoy such familiar pastimes as chariot races and games in the recently enlarged Hippodrome (right). Despite Constantine's conversion to Christianity, pagan belief and ritual were slow to disappear from his dominions; two bronze votive objects (left) made in Constantinople during his rule combine both Christian and pagan symbols.

installed, usually alongside it. The roof, as a rule, was of timber. Such was the general plan of the churches erected by Constantine in this last phase of classical antiquity. A secular counterpart was the grand basilica that he built at this time as a senate house.

Of the churches, the first was that of Hagia Irene, the Holy Peace. It stood on the same spot that a temple of Aphrodite had once occupied — a spot occupied today by a sixth-century Byzantine structure. The adjoining site was designated for the first church of Hagia Sophia, the Holy Wisdom, planned by Constantine but built by his son and successor, Constantius II. Constantine is said to have built other churches on the various hills, but his principal work of ecclesiastical architecture was the Church of the Holy Apostles, which surmounted the fourth hill. It became the official imperial church, the "Westminster Abbey" of the Byzantine emperors, and was designed to serve as their ultimate place of burial.

Constantine's city was later to become rich in Christian relics, largely through the initial example of the emperor's mother, Saint Helena of York. A royal concubine — possibly of Bithynian origin; possibly, as Gibbon declares, the daughter of an English innkeeper — Helena was sanctified by her son, who gave her the title of Augusta, inscribed her effigy on his coinage, named the chief square of his capital the Augustaeum in her honor, and erected in its center a porphyry column with her statue atop it.

In about 325 the emperor sent his mother on a pilgrimage to Jerusalem. Despite her advanced years, Helena made the journey to the Holy Land "with youthful alacrity" and "a truly imperial solicitude." She resolved, in the words of the historian Eusebius, "to discharge the duties of pious devotion to the Supreme God, feeling it incumbent on her to render thanksgivings with prayers on behalf both of her own son, now so mighty an emperor, and of his sons, her own grandchildren, the divinely favored Caesars." Before returning, she erected two basilicas, one on the Mount of Olives and the other over the grotto at Bethlehem where Christ was born; both were destined to become places of Christian pilgrimage. Legend relates that she also carried out excavations on the site of Calvary, and discovered — with divine aid — the True Cross, the crosses of the two thieves, the lance, the sponge, the Crown of Thorns, and other relics of the Passion. Helena's remarkable "finds" were sent home, and Constantinople soon gained a reputation unprecedented in the history of Christendom as a guardian city of sacred relics. The city thus aspired to be not merely the New Rome but the New Jerusalem.

The construction of the city — by a labor force that is said to have included skilled stonecutters from Naples and 40,000 Gothic troops — was expedited by Constantine "with the impatience of a lover." The task took some six years to complete, and the new capital was dedicated in a splendid ceremony on May 11, 330. The inaugural procession, composed of priests, senators, and imperial dignitaries, moved from the west of the city to the Forum of Constantine. A statue of the emperor in the guise of Apollo the sun-god was then heaved on top of the central column to the chanting of Kyrie Eleison. A priest proclaimed the new name of the capital as Constantinopolis, and the city was saluted with acclamations while all the priests cried aloud:

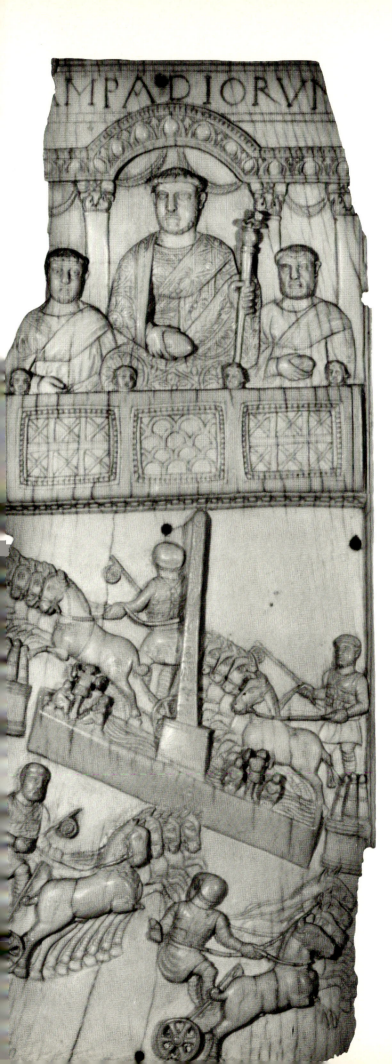

"O Lord guide it on the good path for infinite ages." This inscription was purportedly placed on the column: "O Christ and Master of the World, to You I now dedicate this subject City, and these Scepters, and the Might of Rome. Protector, save her from all harm."

The Christian ceremony was followed by games in the Hippodrome and other, more pagan celebrations. A carved and gilded wooden statue of Constantine holding a figure of Tyche, the city's lucky emblem, in his hand was borne in procession in a triumphal chariot of the sun. A detachment of soldiers carried candles in the wake of the glittering statue, which was placed before the imperial box to receive the emperor's salute. From his throne, Constantine decreed that such ceremonies be repeated on each anniversary of the city's inauguration, and this was done annually for many centuries to come.

Constantine died seven years later. By "slow and almost imperceptible gradations," as Gibbon puts it, he had "declared himself the protector and at length the proselyte of the Church." The approach of death banished further delay and equivocation. During his last illness, he requested and received from his bishops the sacrament of baptism. Insisting that the remainder of his life would be worthy of a disciple of Christ, Constantine humbly refused to wear the imperial purple after he had been clothed in the white garment of a neophyte. He was buried in the mausoleum he had built for the Twelve Apostles — and for his successors — on the fourth hill of his city, and henceforth he was venerated as the Thirteenth Apostle.

It thus was Constantius II who built the first great church of Hagia Sophia — although his father may

Constantinople, the New Rome, inherited both the ecclesiastical preeminence of the Old and the responsibility for resolving doctrinal disputes within the Church. In 381 Theodosius I convened the Council of Constantinople to settle the long-standing feud between the Orthodox and Arian factions over the nature of the Trinity. In the sadly mutilated ninth-century illumination at left Theodosius and the church elders meet in the presence of the enthroned Book of the Evangelists. Below, the emperor greets Saint Gregory of Nazianzus, Patriarch of Constantinople and leader of the triumphant Orthodox cause; at bottom, Orthodox Christians flee the Arian heretics.

have laid its foundations. Adjoining the church of Hagia Irene, which was largely Constantine's work, the new church of the Holy Wisdom fronted on the Augustaeum. A stone basilica of medium size, roofed with timber, it had a nave and four aisles. This first structure was enclosed within a precinct wall, and recent excavations suggest that its orientation corresponded to that of the present church, which faces east with its entrance on the west.

The "great church," as it came to be called even as it took shape before the eyes of the people, was inaugurated on February 15, 360, thirty years after the inauguration of the city. Later it was dedicated to the Holy Wisdom of Christ. It was enriched by the new emperor with treasures of gold and silver: ". . . many tissues adorned with gold thread and stones for the sanctuary; for the doors of the church different curtains of gold; and for the outside gateways many others with gold threads."

This first basilica of Hagia Sophia was the scene of dramatic vicissitudes generated by the religious strife that beset the Byzantine Empire throughout the fourth and fifth centuries. Ironically, the early Christians survived persecution by the pagans only to be torn by equally violent internal conflicts. These had their roots in the need to reconcile, in theological terms, the sophistication of Greco-Roman philosophy with the more rigid ideology of Oriental beliefs, which were largely Semitic in character. Doctrinal warfare raged for centuries over abstract points of dogma that were dear to the minds of theologians, philosophers, and metaphysicians. Increasingly, however, such debates were turned to political account, stirring the religious pas-

In 404 the first Church of Hagia Sophia — built less than fifty years earlier by Constantius II — was damaged by fires set by zealous partisans of John Chrysostom, Patriarch of Constantinople, who had been exiled for his outspoken denunciations of the licentious imperial court. In the glittering miniature at right — from a copy of his Homilies *made more than six centuries after his death — Saint John offers a collection of his sermons to Nicephorus III Botaniates. To the emperor's left is the archangel Michael; the tiny figure at his feet is purportedly that of the artist.*

sions of a populace that was already highly zealous in its outlook. "The subtleties of the Platonic school," writes Gibbon, "were used as the badges of popular factions, and the distance which separated their respective tenets was enlarged or magnified by the acrimony of dispute."

The chief dispute concerned the exact nature of the Holy Trinity, and sought in particular to define the essence of its Second Person, the relation of Son to Father. To what degree was Christ divine, to what degree human? Such questions were passionately debated in fourth-century Constantinople. As Saint Gregory of Nyssa records, it was a time when the city was "full of mechanics and slaves who are all of them profound theologians, and they preach in the shops and the streets. If you want a man to change a piece of money for you, he informs you of in what the Son differs from the Father; if you ask the price of a loaf you are told by way of reply that the Son is inferior to the Father; and if you enquire whether the bath is ready, the answer is that the Son was begotten out of nothing."

Heresies proliferated, among them that of Arius, who maintained that only God was divine; he won fervent public support for his doctrine of "subordination" of Son to Father. The Orthodox doctrine was that of "consubstantiation," accepting a like degree of divinity between Father and Son among the Three Persons of the Trinity. Such was the view adopted by Constantine — who was no theologian, but rather a statesman seeking unity within his empire — at the Council of Nicaea in 325. This, the first of seven councils of the Church convened over the next five centuries, anathematized Arius and propounded the Nicene Creed.

But Constantine's successor, Constantius II, reversed official policy and adopted Arianism. For this he was strongly condemned by the fourth-century pagan historian Ammianus Marcellinus:

> Instead of reconciling the parties by the weight of his authority, he cherished and propagated, by verbal disputes, the differences which his vain curiosity had excited. The highways were covered with troops of bishops, galloping from every side to the assemblies, which they called synods; and while they laboured to reduce the whole sect to their own particular opinions, the public establishments of the posts was almost ruined by their hasty and repeated journeys.

Under the aegis of Constantius the Arian faction, which had tried repeatedly to depose the Orthodox Patriarch Paul in defiance of strong popular protest, finally succeeded in smuggling him out of the city and into exile. An Arian rival was enthroned in Paul's place and was driven from the palace to Hagia Sophia in a chariot flanked by guards with drawn swords. This spectacle inflamed the populace, which surged toward the entrance of Hagia Sophia, creating a panic in which more than three thousand were trampled to death in the square outside.

The reign of Constantius saw, for the first time, the persecution of Christians by other Christians. A reaction toward paganism followed, leading to the accession as emperor of Constantius's uncle and brother-in-law, Julian the Apostate. Julian restored the old gods, reopened temples, and demolished churches. "To be sure," he remarked of Hagia Sophia, "the Christians have a magnificent church. On my return from Persia

I will turn the central space into a hay mow and the aisles into horse stalls. Then I will see upon what they set their faith." Happily he did not carry out his threat.

Julian sought to destroy Christianity by tolerating its two factions and pitting them one against the other. But it was too late to set back the clock. Not long after his death in battle a new Christian dynasty redeemed the excesses of Julian's two-year reign and those of his predecessor. Peace and unity were restored to the church by the propagation, under Theodosius the Great, of a new Orthodox doctrine that reconciled the moderate Arians to the Nicene Creed. Thus Arianism died away and doctrinal peace reigned until a later series of controversies revived religious strife.

It was, rather, a moral and social issue that led to the destruction of the roof of the original Hagia Sophia by fire in 404. A turbulent reforming priest, Saint John Chrysostom, the Patriarch of Constantinople, had been denouncing both the vice and luxury of the imperial court and the immorality of the female sex in the sermons that he delivered from the pulpit of Hagia Sophia. He even compared Empress Eudoxia to Jezebel, and for this and other reasons he was arrested and banished — only to return, following a popular demonstration, to his church. This time he compared her to Herodias demanding the head of Saint John. Riots followed the Easter baptisms, the clergy were driven out, Saint John Chrysostom was exiled, and his partisans set fire to Hagia Sophia. John attributed the fire to supernatural origins, and the saint's biographer Palladius wrote: "Then a flame seemed to burst from the center of the throne in which he used to sit, and climbed up by the chains [of the lamps] to the roof . . . and crept like a

The personification of Constantinople, a crowned female bearing a cornucopia, is a familiar figure in Byzantine art. She appears on a coin (right) minted in 330 — the year that Constantine dedicated his new capital — and again on a fifth-century ivory diptych panel (left).
  Overleaf:
In the sixth century the historian Procopius wrote that Hagia Sophia "soars to a height to match the sky, and, like a ship riding at anchor, higher than the other buildings, it looks down upon the remainder of the city." Fourteen hundred years later, the structure still matches that description and dominates the urban sprawl of modern Istanbul.

wriggling snake upon the back of the church." The senate house was also burned, and "the fire spared only the little house in which the sacred vessels were kept."

Hagia Sophia was rebuilt and rededicated by Theodosius II, with the consecration of new relics. Pulcheria, who reigned conjointly with her brother Theodosius and later reigned alone as empress, dedicated an altar of gold and precious stones to the church on behalf of her virginity and her brother's empire. Theodosius was ruthless in his treatment of the pagans, and by 438 he was able to claim that paganism had been extinguished throughout his empire.

The restored Hagia Sophia was to stand intact for more than a century. Then, on the Ides of January 532, early in the reign of the most famous of all Byzantine emperors, Justinian the Great, it was burned to the ground along with Hagia Irene and other public buildings. This tragic conflagration was touched off by insurgents whom Procopius describes as "some men of the common herd, all the rubbish of the city." These rebels, who raged throughout Constantinople for a frenzied week of fire and bloodshed, took as their rallying cry the Greek word *"nika,"* meaning "conquer." As a result, their rebellion became known as the Nika Riot.

The trouble had started in the Hippodrome, the popular heart of the city. There the charioteers and circus performers — sport heroes like the baseball and football players of our time — were traditionally grouped into two rival factions, the Blues and the Greens. Over the years these factions had evolved into the equivalent of political parties. As a rule, the emperor found it easy to maintain his own power by playing one off against the other, but occasionally the Blues and Greens united. The rivals had done so under Theodosius II, for example. On that occasion their reconciliation had been effected for the constructive purpose of extending and strengthening the walls of the city after an earthquake. (The defenses they erected were to survive all assaults for a thousand years.) Now they united once again, this time in a destructive mood. Under pressure of heavy taxation, corruption, and general discontent, they joined forces in order to depose Justinian.

While the fire raged, Justinian went in person to the Hippodrome, hoping to appease the angry mob with a repentant speech. When his words failed to impress the angry crowd, the emperor's confidence faltered. Uncertain what action to take, he turned to his strong-minded wife, Theodora, who fortified his resolve with the exhortation: "If there were left to me no other safety but in flight," she declared, "I would not fly. Those who have worn the crown should never survive its loss. Never will I see the day that I am not hailed Empress. If you wish to fly, Caesar, well and good; you have money, the ships are ready, the sea is clear; but I shall stay. For I love the old proverb that says, 'The purple is the best winding-sheet.'"

Order was finally restored by the army, which put the mob to rout, leaving 30,000 corpses on the floor of the Hippodrome. Justinian's rule was secure, but Hagia Sophia lay in ruins. Here was a supreme challenge for Justinian the Builder. It became his ambition to create a mightier church. As Procopius observed: "God permitted them to accomplish this impiety, foreseeing into what an object of beauty this shrine was destined to be transformed."

27

II
Church of the Holy Wisdom

The building of the new Hagia Sophia began on February 23, 532, a mere thirty-nine days after the burning of the old. But it is likely that plans for so vast and complex a structure were already at hand, together with a preliminary assembly of marble and other building materials. From the time of his accession five years earlier, the Emperor Justinian had been evolving ambitious architectural plans for his capital, plans designed to ensure his temporal power and immortal fame. He took a personal hand in the conception and construction of the church that was to be Constantinople's cardinal monument; indeed, it was generally believed that its very form had been revealed to the emperor in a dream. And when the site had been measured out and the shape of the dome had been traced, Justinian called upon the patriarch to pray to God for safe building. Then he personally laid the central foundation stone.

In the wake of the fire, the emperor had ordered the ground to be cleared and houses to be purchased for demolition where necessary. Stories were told of imperial bargaining with difficult customers, among them a widow named Anna who balked at the offered price and agreed to relinquish her house only when approached by the emperor himself. She asked no compensation other than her just reward on the Day of Judgment — and burial in a tomb near the church, so that "the memory of her gift might live forever."

There was also a eunuch named Antiochus, "an eager frequenter of the Circus," who refused to sell until imprisoned on the opening day of the games. In return for his release, the eunuch promised to do the emperor's bidding and was conveyed to his empty seat.

There he was obliged to complete his deed of sale before the games could begin, "the Quaestor and the whole Senate being witness." Finally, there was a cobbler named Xenophon who asked for and received twice what his house was worth. He then demanded that the four charioteers of the four factions in the games should do obeisance to him, as they did to the emperor. "The Emperor," an anonymous recorder declares, "decreed that it should be done as he had asked, but made him a laughing stock for ever. For on the day of the games he was set midway in the boundaries, so that the charioteers, by way of a joke, bowed to his back before beginning their courses."

For the work of construction, Procopius writes, the emperor gathered "all the artisans from the whole world." There were some one hundred foremen, each with a hundred men beneath him. Justinian shrewdly split his work force in two, with fifty foremen and their staffs working on the right half of the church and fifty on the left, so that the structure rose rapidly in a spirit of zealous competition. Within two years it had already risen as high as the first story of the side aisles. The labor force, apart from manual workers on the site and in the brickyards and quarries, included a high proportion of skilled workers, among them the leaders of many organized crafts or guilds. Stonecutters, masons, carpenters, polishers, and workers in iron, bronze, and lead were engaged, and as the work proceeded they were joined by sculptors, marbleworkers, mosaicists, goldsmiths, and glassblowers.

The chief architect was Anthemius of Tralles, whom Procopius describes as "the most learned man in the skilled craft which is known as the art of building";

his assistant was "another master-builder, Isidorus by name, a Milesian by birth, a man who was intelligent and worthy to assist the Emperor Justinian." Both were Greeks from Asia Minor. Anthemius, we are told by Agathias, another contemporary writer, "was the one who thought out everything and carried it through." Skilled, like Isidorus, in mathematics and kindred sciences, he came from a talented family that included a philologist, a jurist, and two important doctors. He is described as a man of many crafts, an inventor, with a reputation for skill in engineering. Anthemius also appears to have been something of a practical joker. According to Agathias, he once concocted an elaborate scheme to frighten a troublesome neighbor who lived on the floor above him. Well-versed in the principles of steam power, he fitted pipes of hide to cauldrons of water that he had secretly installed in his room. He then lit fires under the cauldrons and steam poured upward, stirring and shaking the ceiling and causing it to tremble. This story, we are told, "is much used by those who declare that the uprising of smoky vapors is the cause of earthquake; and quite rightly, for the engineer, they say, recognizing the cause whereby it comes about that the earth is shaken, did reproduce it, and by his art did mimic nature."

Justinian regularly supervised the construction work, and he was ever ready to give advice to the architects. Procopius records an occasion when piers began to crack under the weight of the incompleted eastern arch, which seemed on the point of collapsing. Anthemius and Isidorus, terrified at what had happened, carried the matter to the emperor, "having come to have no hope in their technical skill. And straightaway

the emperor, impelled by I know not what, but I suppose by God (for is he not himself a master-builder?) commanded them to carry the curve of this arch to its final completion. 'For when it rests upon itself,' he said, 'it will no longer need the props beneath it.'" This was done, and the arch was completed without further incident. On another occasion some columns began to throw off tiny flakes when a load of masonry was placed on top of them. The emperor sensibly attributed this to the dampness of parts of the masonry, and on his advice it was removed and replaced when it had dried.

Justinian spent much of his time on the site. Part of a *metatorium*, or imperial retiring room, was built so that he could eat and rest during the day, and then a portico was added "so that, as often as he liked, he might cross over and devote his time to the building, without being seen by anyone" — or so legend relates. On his visits to the site the emperor wore a white linen garment, with a kerchief over his head, and carried a stick in his hand. The workmen were paid by the imperial treasurer daily from a store of money deposited at the sundial, "and each of those who carried stone received a piece of silver, lest any slackness should come upon them, or they should be tempted to complain." To encourage the workmen, a heap of coins was mixed with the earth each day, and in the evening when work was done they were allowed to forage for them, digging for what they could find.

The building of the church was attended, it seems, by a series of miraculous manifestations. It became a legend in later centuries that "an angel of God appeared and taught the workmen as they were building."

The damaged manuscript below depicts Emperor
Justinian supervising the construction of Hagia
Sophia. That phenomenal task was completed
only five years after the earlier church on the site
had been destroyed by fire in 532.

And it is recorded that one Sunday, when the laborers had left the worksite to go home for their dinners, they left a boy of fourteen there to guard their tools. The apparition of a eunuch materialized before him, "clad in shining garments, and fair to look upon, like one sent from the palace," and asked him "why the workmen do not quickly finish the work of God, but have left it and gone to eat?" The boy replied that they would soon be back. The eunuch commanded him: "Go quickly and summon them here, for I swear to thee, my son, by the Holy Wisdom, whose temple is now being built, I will not depart, since, by the command of the Word of God, I am to minister and guard here until you return."

The boy's father promptly took him to the emperor, who commanded all his eunuchs to appear before the youth. When he identified none of them, "the emperor knew that it was an angel of the Lord who had addressed the boy," and he "praised God, saying 'God has accepted my temple.'" He would not allow the boy to go back to the church, "so that the angel may guard it for ever, as he promised by his oath. For if the boy returns, the angel will depart." The principal senators and bishops concurred with the emperor, "so that, by the grace of God, it should have a guardian till the end of the world." The boy meanwhile was "loaded with gifts and honors" and sent to the Cyclades.

When the inner sanctuary was being built there was disagreement between Justinian and his builders as to whether its apse should have one window or two. This matter was reportedly settled when an angel of the Lord appeared, dressed like the emperor with royal robes and shoes, and said to the craftsmen, "I will that there be a triple light, and that the conch be made with three windows in the name of the Father, the Son, and the Holy Ghost." The emperor, who had not left his palace all day, knew that this was a miraculous visitation and therefore informed his builders, "As I have bidden thee, so do."

Such legends grew and multiplied through the centuries. A thirteenth-century Arab traveler wrote of the church, ". . . they say one of the angels resides there; round about this place they have made fences of gold." At this same time a Russian monk declared that the Virgin herself had been seen in the sanctuary one night by a priest. Sir John Mandeville, the fourteenth-century traveler, related that once when a grave was made in the church, "they found a body in the earth, and upon the body lay a plate of gold, that said thus in Hebrew, Greek, and Latin, 'Jesus Christ shall be born of the Virgin Mary, and I believe in Him.' It was laid there 2000 years before the birth of Christ, and is still preserved in the treasury of the Church."

Justinian built his church regardless of expense. A timely addition to his funds came from the confiscated estates of senators involved in the Nika Riot, but such sums were only a fraction of the total cost, which Gibbon estimates was the equivalent of $2,000,000. Later estimates, allowing for the cost of the gold, precious stones, crosses, sacred vessels, lamps, ornaments, and other treasures, vary between the equivalent of $75,000,000 and $150,000,000 in modern currency. According to an anonymous chronicler, "the revenues of 365 farms in Egypt, India, and all the East and West were devoted to the maintenance of the Church. For each holy day was set aside 1,000 measures of oil, 300 meas-

In 558, twenty-one years after the consecration of
Hagia Sophia, the hastily built dome was toppled
by an earthquake. The reconstructed semispherical
dome (right) is pierced by forty arched windows.
Clearly visible in the interior view at left are the
mosaics that decorate its center.

ures of wine, and 1,000 sacramental loaves."

Hagia Sophia, with all its decoration and ornament, was finished in the short space of five years, ten months, and four days. The building itself was a unique architectural creation. It fused the ideas of imperial Rome with those of Christian Byzantium, and for the first time it achieved for Christian architecture "a truly monumental form." Its design marked the decline of the basilica and the ascendancy of the dome. Over the centuries, the dome set on a circular building — such as the Pantheon in Rome — had evolved into the dome set on a square, reduced to an octagon and supported by a circle of arches. In Constantinople, it evolved into its final stage, the true dome, which rested on the summits of four arches above four piers and was completed at the corners by four triangular, curved pendentives.

The great dome of Hagia Sophia is supported by a combination of barrel vaults and half domes. The church provides, in the words of E. H. Swift, "an exposition of the potentialities of the arch, with its derivatives the vault and the dome, undreamed of by the earlier architects of imperial Rome." In this sense, the evolution of the dome as a unifying architectural feature seems to derive from the East. The architects of Hagia Sophia were Greeks from Asia Minor, thus subject to influences not merely Hellenistic but Oriental. It was this synthesis that inspired them to construct the church's "huge spherical dome," which, in the words of Procopius, "seems not to rest on solid masonry, but to cover the space with its golden dome suspended from Heaven."

Space is indeed the essential element in the architectural conception of Hagia Sophia. Here are spatial principles developed as never before, space floating in vistas, rising vertically, expanding horizontally — a rhythm of voids concealing the function of the solid elements and creating a light, open, flowing construction. Here is a spatial effect that Thomas Whittemore, the church's modern restorer, liked to define — with a wave of the hand that gave a poetical lilt to his technical jargon — as "volumetric."

Hagia Sophia is no cruciform church, like those of the Christian West, but a domed Christian basilica on a centralized plan. Evolved from the Roman rectangular form, it is a square within a rectangle that is itself almost square, its main floor measuring 220 by 250 feet. The four arches of its nave rise to a height of 70 feet, and the dome resting on them rises to a total height of 180 feet. Forty ribs and curved webs radiate from the center of the dome to 40 windows at its outside rim, whose diameter is more than 100 feet. Two half domes cover the niches to east and west that serve respectively as the apse and the entrance bay. They too are pierced with rounded windows and matched by many more in the flat tympana that fill the arches to the north and south. Beneath the tympana, flanking the nave, are the colonnades of two broad, vaulted side aisles that rise in two tiers, the upper tier making "fair upper galleries for the women." Such is the ordered "shell," curvilinear and vertical, enclosing the great volume of space that expands and spreads, as it were, in its own weightless spherical element.

The form of the church was dictated by the form of the Greek liturgy. For its sacred and dramatic impact, this demanded a nave that was in effect a wide open "stage." It was reserved for the public moments of the

Mass by the patriarch and his priesthood, who symbolized respectively the hierarch and the celestial hierarchies of the angels. On saints' days and other church festivals, the emperor, when present with his court, was the sole lay participant, echoing in his prayers a hymn of thanksgiving offered to God by King David. The rest of the congregation gathered in the broad side aisles beyond the colonnades and in the galleries above them. (In Western churches the nave, or the long western arm of a cruciform building, would be designed specifically for worshipers.)

Except at certain moments — such as at the Lesser Entrance, or initial procession into the sanctuary, and the Great Entrance, introduced by Justinian, in which the priests proceeded around the nave with the elements of the Eucharist, reciting prayers and preceded by acolytes with lighted tapers — the congregation saw relatively little of the sacred ritual. For the Divine Liturgy itself was enacted as a Great Mystery, invisible behind the screen and the drawn curtains of the sanctuary. The emperor, who had entered the church with the patriarch, sat with his courtiers in the imperial enclosure. Periodically the patriarch and his clergy would enter the open expanse of the nave to read the scriptures, preach a sermon from the pulpit, exchange the Kiss of Peace with the emperor, or administer to him the elements of the Holy Communion.

Only when the clergy and the emperor had completed their roles beneath the dome did the congregation move into the nave to receive the bread and the wine themselves. This act of participation following the ritual of the liturgy symbolized for the citizen of Constantinople his brotherhood in a community at once

divine and imperial. It was here in the great nave that the "two halves of God," the respective hierarchies of patriarch and clergy, emperor and court, converged.

The church was an embodiment not only of space but of light. Light poured down from the massive dome to make an open, luminous space of the central nave beneath. From the shadows of the side aisles the faithful could gaze in wonder, entranced by the divine radiance that shone beyond and above and, when the time came to move forward, directly and individually upon them. Symbolic or otherwise, the lighting of Hagia Sophia was of fabulous brilliance. By day the church was flooded diagonally with sunlight from the host of lunettes and round-headed windows. By night its artificial illumination was comparable to that of a midnight sun.

Inside the great church the light was diffused by thousands of lamps and candelabra at differing levels. Chains of beaten brass fell from the rim of the dome, "linked in alternating curves with many windings" and terminating at some height above the floor in a great metal circle. From this hung silver disks containing glass oil vases and crosses of metal that likewise bore lamps. Together they formed a coronet above the heads of the congregation, a circling chorus of bright lights.

Along the sides of the church were rows of lamps, mostly of silver, set at differing levels. "From twisted chains," wrote Paul the Silentiary, "they sweetly flash in their aerial courses, even as shines twin-pointed Hyas fixed in the forehead of Taurus. One might also see ships of silver, bearing a flashing freight of flame, and plying their lofty courses in the liquid air instead of the sea." The base of the "deep-bosomed dome" had its

Viewed from this unusual perspective, the huge dome of Hagia Sophia appears even higher than its actual 180 feet above the pavement of the nave.

own source of light, for along the projecting stone of the curved cornice the skillful workmen had suspended single lamps from bronze stakes.

The lightness and brightness of Hagia Sophia were enhanced by the gold mosaic that covered the ceiling of the dome and the surfaces of the vaults and arches — four acres of it in all. This glitter was further enhanced by the gleam and polish of the stones that shone from the floors and the walls, for Justinian had procured marble and other fine stones from all parts of his empire — and even from as far afield as the Atlantic coast of France. In response to an imperial command, provincial officials had ransacked public baths, private houses, and the shrines of pagan idols for stone. Nearer home, the quarries and marble workshops of Marmara Island were employed to furnish cornices, capitals, and plaques.

In the face of such splendor the Silentiary rhapsodized: "Who, even in the measures of Homer, shall sing the marble pastures gathered on the lofty walls and spreading pavement of the mighty church? These the iron with its metal tooth has gnawed — the fresh green from Carystus, and many-colored marble from the Phrygian range, in which a rosy blush mingles with white, or it shines bright with flowers of deep red and silver." There was, he added, a wealth of porphyry from Egypt, emerald from Sparta, and glittering marble from the Jassian hills with its slanting streaks of blood red and white.

As Procopius expressed it, he who entered Hagia Sophia might imagine that he had come upon a meadow with its flowers in full bloom. He would surely marvel at the purple of some surfaces, the green tint of others:

". . . at those on which the crimson glows and those from which the white flashes, and again at those which Nature, like some painter, varies with the most contrasting colors."

Columns abound in the structure of Hagia Sophia: in all there are 104 monoliths, 40 in the nave and 64 in the triforium. The nave is flanked by eight green marble columns from the quarries of Thessaly. These are not strictly vertical, but taper imperceptibly upward, creating one of those optical illusions familiar in various parts of the church. Eight shafts of porphyry, almost as large, rise to form the semicircular colonnades that round off the arcades of the nave. In the age of Procopius they tilted inward in a semicircular pattern "as if they were yielding to one another in a choral dance." These monoliths came from the renowned quarries of the porphyry mountain near Thebes, in Upper Egypt, and were believed to have once stood in the Temple of the Sun at Ba'albek. A later and doubtless equally apocryphal tale identifies them as part of the dowry of a Roman widow named Marcia who supposedly wrote to the emperor: "I send unto you columns of equal length, weight, and thickness, for the salvation of my soul." Small crosses of consecration, probably carved by the builders and later inlaid with metal, have been sunk into a number of columns. In others, only the sunken panels remain where the Turks pried out the crosses.

On the far side of the aisles stand twenty-four smaller monoliths — sixteen of green marble and cylindrical, eight of white marble and rectangular. Flanking the triforium are thirty-six smaller columns of green marble; an additional twenty-four columns of white marble

Seen in semishadow, the rising tiers of columns and windows that flank the nave (right) create an aura of inviting mystery. The monogram of the church's builder, Justinian, is set within the intricate patterns of acanthus leaves that adorn the capital of the massive pillar at left.

are set within it. There is little uniformity of height and thickness among all these columns, derived as they are from so many sources. The discrepancy has been concealed by various expedients, notably the use of bases and capitals of varying size and form. "And the lofty crest of every column," writes Paul the Silentiary, ". . . is covered with many a supple curve of waving acanthus — a wandering chain of barbed points all golden, full of grace. Thus the marble in bulging forms crowns the deep red columns, as wool the distaff; the stone glittering with a beauty that charms the heart." These capitals, often with crosses or imperial monograms, are indeed masterpieces of Byzantine stonecutting at its richest. Their designs, with filigree as fine as lacework, embody not only the acanthus but tendrils and scrolls, basketwork, spirals, and other patterns of more abstract character. Many were originally picked out in gold leaf against a deep blue ground.

Sacred significance was attached to specific marble slabs whose veins formed lifelike shapes — the likeness, for example, of a bearded human head crowned with a helmet or the bust of a woman with hands uplifted in prayer. One was said to resemble Saint John the Baptist, another "the holy Virgin Mary, with our Lord Jesus Christ in her most holy arms." Such slabs, framed as panels within beaded moldings, were used as a revetment to sheathe the walls. Selectively matched and brightly polished, they were rich in a variety of natural patterns and colors — greens and whites, reds and purples and yellows. Sometimes they were successive slices cut from a single block of marble, repeating one another to make continuous, symmetrical designs, and thus marrying nature with art. "The gleam

of the stones," Procopius writes, "is surpassing, outshining that of gold." This form of wall decoration is characteristically Byzantine, and may be compared to the Oriental practice of covering mud-brick walls with carpets, tapestries, and other such hangings.

The floors of the church were as generously paved with marble: "Gladly have the hills of Proconnesus bent their backs to necessity. In parts too shimmers the polish of the Bosporus stone, with white streaks on black." Echoing the Silentiary, an anonymous chronicler compares the shimmer of "huge white slabs" to "that of the sea or to the flowing water of rivers." These strips had a symbolic and ritualistic rather than a decorative purpose. In the exact center of the nave was the *omphalos*, the "navel" of the earth. It was a piece of inlaid pavement, resembling one that survives in the southeastern part of the nave and takes the form of a large disk of dark marble within a square frame. Surrounding it are smaller disks of red marble, each on a ground of green with mosaic ornament and each encircled by a band of Proconnesian marble. The medieval Russian monk Anthony of Novgorod describes "a slab of red marble upon which they set a golden throne whereon they crown the emperor. And a [rail of] bronze surrounds this place, that no man may tread upon it; but the folk worship it, for here did the All-Holy Virgin pray to her Son our Lord on behalf of all Christians."

Commanding the east end of the church, and providing the scene for the hidden drama of the Divine Liturgy, was the chancel known as the bema — a Holy of Holies into which no layman except the emperor, with his semipriestly status as the Thirteenth Apostle, might

Justin II continued the work begun by his uncle and predecessor, Justinian, by sponsoring many of the original nonfigural wall mosaics in Hagia Sophia. He also commissioned the silver gilt cross at right as a gift for the pope. The figure of Jesus appears in the upper and lower medallions; in the center is the Agnus Dei, the lamb with cross and halo that is a symbol of Christ.

enter. Before it, "like an island rising from the sea," was the towering ambo, a circular pulpit of stone mounted by two flights of steps. Here the Gospel was read, prayers recited, and important offices during coronations performed. The original ambo was said to have had columns and a dome of solid gold studded with precious stones, and its floor was supposedly paved with sardonyx.

Leading from the ambo to the bema was the solea, a passageway with a balustrade "prolonged like an isthmus, wave-washed on either side," that led the priest from the distant ambo to the shrine of the Holy Table. It passed through the "throng of the choir," where men and boys sang *a capella* lyrical hymns and responses in glorification of God. (One such hymn, "Christ the Only-Begotten Son," is said to have been written by Justinian, who loved music.)

The solea led to the three Holy Doors of the iconostasis, which screened the sanctuary itself. Through these gates only the clergy and the emperor, with acolytes, might pass. The screen, as described in its rebuilt form by the Silentiary, was plated with silver, and its columns were likewise "sheathed with the silver metal, even six sets of twain; and the rays of light glitter far and wide."

Behind the silver screen, on the platform of the bema, was the "all gold slab of the Holy Table, standing on gold foundations, and bright with the glitter of different stones." "Who," cries the anonymous chronicler, "can see the Holy Table without being astonished? and who can gaze on it on account of the many glinting surfaces? so that at one time it all appears of gold; from another place all of silver, and in another

of glittering sapphire." This brilliant effect, he writes, was achieved by Justinian's craftsmen after consultation with the emperor. At his suggestion they "cast into the melting pot gold, silver, stones of every kind, and pearls, copper, electron, lead, tin, iron, glass, and every other metallic substance. And they ground them all together and formed them into masses, and poured them into the pot; and when it had been melted, they took it from the fire and poured it out into a mold. Thus the Holy Table was made."

Above the table — and covering the elements of the Eucharist — stood the canopied shrine of the ciborium, "reared in fourfold arches of silver . . . borne aloft on silver columns," surmounted by an octagonal silver cone and, on the top of that, a globe with a cross. At Justinian's command, five gold crosses were made, each weighing a hundred pounds and each encrusted with precious stones. Two gold candlesticks were similarly adorned, as were two candelabra with golden feet, and "fifty others too, of silver, the height of a man, to stand by the altar." Roughly $240,000 was spent on the adornment of the ambo and solea — a sum derived, according to the anonymous chronicler, by levying tribute on the Persians, among others.

Beneath the cross on the ciborium the emperor suspended, from the center of the canopy, a crown and a dove of gold. Crowns multiplied as the centuries passed, and eventually the church was enriched by as many as thirty. These, together with the jeweled crosses, reliquaries, and gold and silver vessels used in the liturgy, were the work of innumerable individual craftsmen and their apprentices, organized in guilds, who flourished in the bazaars of Constantinople.

Hanging along the four sides of the ciborium were altar curtains made from woven silk. Elsewhere throughout the church were other silk hangings — veils over the doors and arcades in figured, heraldic, or geometrical patterns. These were products of the silk-weaving industry that Justinian founded in Constantinople after two visiting Chinese divulged the secret of raising silkworms to him.

The bema was flanked by two side chambers. To the north lay the prothesis, where the elements of the sacrament were set forth; to the south lay the vestry, where the robes of the priests were kept. Behind it, to the east, was the apse with its concentric tiers of seats for the clergy, which widened at each higher level to become a semicircle of resplendent silver stalls. The entrance to the church was through the atrium (of which few traces now remain), an open arcaded courtyard at Hagia Sophia's western end, facing the great square of the Augustaeum. The atrium was paved with marble and surrounded by cloisters on three sides. In its center stood a fountain at which the devout washed their feet before entering the shrine.

The fourth side of the courtyard formed the outer narthex. It opened into the narthex itself, the internal "porch" of the church, through five doorways of which the largest was the imperial entrance. The narthex, which survives, appeared to the Silentiary to be "as long as the wondrous church is broad." It is, in fact, a long rectangle, relatively shallow in width but lofty in height. With its high marbled walls, its leaping arches, and its flashing gold mosaic cross vaults ornamented in various colors, the narthex prepares the eye for the unrestricted space and the splendor of the nave beyond. Of the nine doorways leading into the body of the church, three monumental royal gates lead directly into the nave. All have jambs and lintels of marble. The marble frame and cornice of the central gate, through which the emperor made his entrance, are sheathed in finely wrought and ornamented bronze that was probably gilded at one time. Above the door is a shallow relief, dating back to the church's foundation, that shows a throne and an open book of the Gospel on which the dove of the Holy Spirit is flying down from Heaven. The inscription on its pages, from the Gospel of Saint John, reads: "The Lord hath said: I am the door of the sheep; by me if any man enter in he shall be saved and shall go in and out, and find pasture."

The wood of these three doors was said to have come from the ark, and to have been sheathed in silver. At one time many of the doors in the church were covered with bronzework, variously and often richly ornamented, then silvered and gilded. Indeed, a thirteenth-century Crusader, Robert of Clari, went so far as to declare that there was no gate in the entire church that was *not* sheathed in silver. The anonymous chronicler describes "carved ivory doors overlaid with gold, to the number of 365." He adds — echoing, as in other passages, biblical accounts of the building of Solomon's Temple — that the emperor wished to pave the floor of the sanctuary with silver, but was dissuaded from doing so by his Greek advisers, for fear that some poorer successor to the imperial throne might tear up the paving and remove it.

Next to the narthex, and outside the body of the church, is the baptistery, a handsome octagonal build-

Three monumental wooden doors in the narthex lead directly into the nave of Hagia Sophia; the central and largest one (below) was reserved exclusively for the emperor. Carved above the door is a shallow relief decoration (close-up at right) of the dove of the Holy Spirit poised atop a throne, on which rests a book open to a passage from the Gospel of Saint John.

ing with a shallow dome and a sunken font. This still survives, although it was probably a second baptistery in the north side that admitted most of the congregation to the fonts.

For all its monumental scale and majestic position, the exterior of Hagia Sophia, open to the heavens, was outshone—as in the case of many Byzantine churches—by the interior, enclosing the heavens. Nonetheless, in its original form — since obscured and confused by buttresses and other later additions — it was a compact, balanced structure, imposing as a group of rising masses and volumes that carried the eye upward in a progression of cylindrical vaults and half domes to the great dome at the summit, all roofed with lead. As it rose, forming a unified whole, it gained in weight and substance from the smooth, static surfaces and the niches bereft of detailed ornament, to the dynamic rounded forms above, swiveling and bulging in rhythmical harmony over the rooftops of the buildings then massed around it. Far from being a mere outer casing for a consummate interior, it embodied a parallel concept of spatial design, free from structural extrusions and achieving a true architectural subtlety.

The interior of the church depended, for its structural and spatial effect, on the four main piers, which were sheathed in marble and thus did not seem to obtrude. Together with four lesser piers they carried the full weight of the dome and its arches. The piers, as Procopius describes them, were "composed of huge stones joined together, carefully selected and fitted to one another, and rising to a great height. One might suppose that they were sheer mountain peaks." He adds that they were held together "neither with lime,

which they call 'asbestos,' nor by asphalt, the material which was the pride of Semiramis in Babylon, nor by any other such thing, but by lead poured into the interstices, which flowed about everywhere in the spaces between the stones and hardened in the joints, binding them to each other." The Silentiary refers to "sheets" of lead and to a cement poured into the joints, that was made of "the dust of fireburnt stone."

The piers were further strengthened by clamps of iron similar to those used in other parts of the church. The masonry used for their construction was a form of ashlar, hewn from a light porous volcanic rock that was adaptable to pressure. Elsewhere throughout the church, the main material used was baked brick; timber was studiously avoided for fear of fire. The bricks were thin, yellowish-red in color, and rested on courses of red mortar of similar thickness.

The construction of a building like Hagia Sophia had never before been considered feasible on so large a scale. It presented a new architectural challenge that required a new type of architect. Such a project was beyond the scope of the master builders who had hitherto designed and constructed most of the imperial buildings, and the emperor chose Anthemius and Isidorus for the task because they had qualifications of a different kind. They were not mere builders, but scholars and mathematicians trained in the theory of statics and dynamics — and, moreover, able to translate them into practice as engineers through training and instructing their team of technicians and craftsmen. The creation of Hagia Sophia was a task that called not merely for the technical skill of the engineer but for the intellectual equipment of the scientist and the

ΟΝ ΑCΜΑ ΚΑΙΝΟΝ· ΑCΑΤΕ
ΤΩ ΚΩ ΠΑCΑ ΗΓΗ·
ΑCΑΤΕ ΤΩ ΚΩ ΕΥΛΟΓΗCΑΤΕ ΤΟ ΟΝΟ
ΜΑ ΑΥΤΟΥ· ΕΥΑΓΓΕΛΙCΑCΘ ΑΙ ΗΜΕΡΑ
ΕΞ ΗΜΕΡΑC ΤΟ CΡΙΟΝ ΑΥΤΟΥ·
ΑΝΑΓΓΕΙΛΑΤΕ ΕΝ ΤΟΙC ΕΘ ΝΕCΙΝ ΤΗ
ΔΟΞΑΝ ΑΥΤΟΥ ΕΝ ΠΑCΙΝ ΤΟΙC ΛΑ
ΟΙC ΤΑ ΘΑΥΜΑCΙΑ ΑΥΤΟΥ·
ΟΤΙ ΜΕΓΑC ΚC ΚΑΙ ΑΙΝΕΤΟC CΦΟΔΡΑ
ΦΟΒΕΡΟC ΕCΤΙΝ ΕΠΙ ΠΑΝΤΑC ΤΟΥC
ΘΕΟΥC·
ΟΤΙ ΠΑΝΤΕC ΟΙ ΘΕΟΙ ΤΩΝ ΕΘ ΝΩΝ
ΔΑΙΜΟΝΙΑ· Ο ΔΕ ΚC ΤΟΥC ΟΥΡΑΝΟΥC
ΕΠΟΙΗCΕΝ·
ΕΞΟΜΟΛΟΓΗCΙC ΚΑΙ ΩΡΑΙΟΤΗC ΕΝΩ
ΠΙΟΝ ΑΥΤΟΥ· ΑΓΙΟCΥΝΗ ΚΑΙ ΜΕ
ΓΑΛΟΠΡΕΠΕΙΑ ΕΝ ΤΩ ΑΓΙΑCΜΑ
ΤΙ ΑΥΤΟΥ·
ΕΝΕΓΚΑΤΕ ΤΩ ΚΩ ΑΙ ΠΑΤΡΙΑΙ ΤΩ
ΕΘ ΝΩΝ· ΕΝΕΓΚΑΤΕ ΤΩ ΚΩ ΔΟ
ΞΑΝ ΚΑΙ ΤΙΜΗΝ·
ΕΝΕΓΚΑΤΕ ΤΩ ΚΩ ΔΟΞΑΝ ΟΝΟΜΑ

imaginative perception of the artist; it called for a man who combined the daring of an innovator with the aesthetic vision of a genius.

Anthemius, though not in the strict sense a trained architect, possessed such qualities. But the theorist and, above all, the artist within him were continually at odds with the practical engineer — and too often defeated him. As an architect his task was fraught with hazards. But with no model of similar scale and complexity to guide him, Anthemius had to experiment, to take risks. The Romans, in attempting such a task, could rely on their own form of concrete, a material rigid enough to counter the various thrusts in the structure. But the Byzantines of the sixth century seem to have lost the art of casting concrete. Thus Anthemius had to build in bricks and mortar, materials too flexible to resist the stresses exerted by the dome on the vaults and the four supporting arches, all of which pushed, as the Silentiary expresses it, "like active demons." These thrusts he had to meet with a variety of counterthrusts — using half domes, buttresses, and other reinforcing devices. Such expedients gave rise to structural faults nonetheless.

In his search as an artist for aesthetic perfection, often at the cost of distortion and dissimulation, Anthemius tended to take liberties as an engineer with the dictates of engineering science. Moreover, the emperor was impatient for him to finish the building on time. The creation of Hagia Sophia may have been attended by miracles, but the chief miracle, as modern writers have dryly observed, was that it stayed up at all.

The sad fact is that it soon toppled. In 553 an earthquake weakened the crown of the eastern arch. Four years later, a second earthquake succeeded in splitting the arch completely. Efforts to repair it were in vain, and five months later, in 558, the arch, part of the eastern semidome, and a large portion of the main dome itself collapsed, destroying as it did so the Holy Table, the ciborium, and the ambo. Describing this catastrophe, the Silentiary writes that "the very foundations of the dome failed, and thick clouds of dust darkened the midday sun. Yet the whole church did not fall. Part lay on the ground, part open to the light of day, hung suspended in the air." The emperor, he tells us, "soon began to build again, the Genius of New Rome by his side."

Both Anthemius and Isidorus were dead — spared the sight of their ruined handiwork — and the work of reconstruction was carried out by Isidorus the Younger, a nephew of the Elder. Attributing the fall to the thrust of the relatively low, flat dome of Anthemius, Isidorus built a new dome, steeper and twenty feet higher than the old. He made other alterations, restoring the piers, broadening the arches. The results were generally reassuring, since the new dome "did not frighten the spectators as formerly, but was set much stronger and safer." Isidorus is reputed also to have added the external tower buttresses to strengthen the piers, but these may well have been built before the first church's completion — as a precaution against structural distortions already evident at that time.

The restored church was reconsecrated in 563 in a processional ceremony. Thus ended the first — and possibly the worst — of many misadventures that were to befall the Church of the Holy Wisdom throughout its long, dramatic, turbulent history.

III
Constantinople's Golden Age

The reign of Justinian marked the climax of Constantinople as the capital of the Eastern Empire. In effect, his rule spanned half the sixth century, for Justinian reigned de facto from 518 to 527 (as adviser and regent for his illiterate uncle Justin) and de jure from 527 until his death in 565 at the age of eighty-two. He saw himself both as the heir of the Caesars and as the elect of God. His self-appointed task was the renewal, in all its ancient power and glory, of the Western Roman Empire, which had fallen under the sway of the barbarians in the century preceding his accession to the imperial throne.

Thanks to Belisarius and other able commanders, Justinian was able to liberate Africa from the Vandals, Italy from the Ostrogoths, and a part of Spain from the Visigoths. He made the Mediterranean a Roman lake once more, almost doubled his territorial possessions, and effectively established Byzantine power throughout the former Western Roman world. He reunited and secured the empire within lines of frontier fortresses that became known as "Justinians."

Despite such precautions, the emperor was obliged to fight a war on two fronts. While his troops were engaged against his various enemies in the West, the Persians began to encroach upon Justinian's eastern provinces. In the course of a five-year campaign the belligerent King Khosrau descended upon Syria, pillaged Antioch, invaded Armenia, and laid waste to Mesopotamia. After a long series of battles on the Euphrates frontier, Justinian was obliged, shortly before his death, to sign a fifty-year treaty that confirmed certain territorial adjustments and obliged him to pay tribute to the Persian king.

Meanwhile a bronze equestrian statue of Justinian in the guise of Achilles was erected in the center of the Augustaeum, opposite Hagia Sophia. According to Procopius, the sculptor depicted the emperor "stretching forth his right hand toward the rising sun, with fingers spread, commanding the barbarians in that quarter to remain at home and advance no further." Raised on a brick column plated with bronze, this effigy seemed to tower above the church itself. In its left hand the figure held a globe from which sprang a cross, symbol of the new Christian culture that had changed the direction of classical civilization in sixth-century Constantinople. Embodied in it was the intellectual tradition of ancient Greece and the military, legal, and administrative traditions of Rome. Thus, before achieving the external renewal of his empire in military terms, Justinian had renewed it internally in terms of the law.

The traditional legal system, inherited from Rome and depending in some degree upon representation of the people, needed revision to accord with the responsibilities of an absolute monarchy. To give his people "definite and indisputable laws," Justinian appointed a commission of jurists to produce a new code. This was followed by a Digest of Roman Jurisprudence, and it by a revised code to which ordinances were added as time went by. This codified legal system adapted the laws of Rome to the new Christian society. Based on the principles of *philanthropia,* or love of the emperor toward mankind, it embodied new conceptions of social justice, public morality, equity, and humanity.

As admirable in intention was Justinian's attempt to reform the civil service, a scheme designed to reduce

corruption, increase salaries, and rationalize administration. Owing to general financial and fiscal confusion, this plan failed to achieve its goals, however. Nonetheless, Justinian could boast with some justification that he had, "by his brilliant ideas, given a new flower to the State."

That flower bloomed most visibly in the emperor's prodigal public works, which brought prestige to the state and to his imperial office. He built innumerable churches throughout his empire. Among the first of these was the Church of Saint Sergius and Saint Bacchus, or "Little Hagia Sophia," in Constantinople. (Built before Hagia Sophia, it was to serve in a sense as its prototype.) Succeeding and adjoining the great church like a satellite was the new Hagia Irene, or Church of the Holy Peace. Justinian also built a new Church of the Holy Apostles, which was to serve as a model for Saint Mark's in Venice. Apart from the churches, Justinian's widespread building program embraced baths, colonnades, aqueducts, cisterns, harbors, roads, and bridges — together with such benefactions as free hospitals. His was indeed the first Golden Age of Constantinople, in all its grandeur and beauty and majesty.

Justinian was known as "the emperor who never slept" — a description not only figurative but literal, if Gibbon is to be believed:

> After repose of a single hour, the body was awakened by the soul, and, to the astonishment of his chamberlains, Justinian walked or studied till the morning light. Such restless application prolonged his time for the acquisition of knowledge and the despatch of business; and he might seriously deserve the reproach of

confounding, by minute and prosperous diligence, the general order of his administration.

Indeed, his nocturnal habits were legendary. His enemies whispered that he was no mere man but an evil spirit who required no rest, and he was said to have been seen prowling through the corridors of his palace without his head. The emperor's diet was abstemious, says Gibbon, regulated "not by the prudence of a philosopher but the superstition of a monk. His repasts were short and frugal . . . and such was his strength, as well as his fervour, that he frequently passed two days and as many nights without tasting any food." His disposition was chaste, and he was faithful to his "sweetest charmer," Theodora.

A "theatrical prostitute," brought up in the world of the circus and skilled in the art of pantomime, Theodora became first the emperor's concubine and then, through a change in the law, his wife. Before her death she was elevated to the rank of empress and co-sovereign, "adored as a queen . . . by grave magistrates, orthodox bishops, victorious generals, and captive monarchs." Procopius wrote that "it was impossible for mere man to describe her comeliness in words, or imitate it in art." Furthermore, she was a woman of resolute will and farsighted intelligence who shared her husband's ruthless ambition and taste for power and who wielded an influence over him which was, on balance, beneficial.

But there was one vital sphere in which the respective paths of the two monarchs diverged — that of religion. As he reconquered the West and defeated the heretical barbarians, Justinian emerged as the great champion of Christian Orthodoxy. During the previous

In addition to Hagia Sophia, Justinian built a new Church of the Holy Apostles in Constantinople. That five-domed cruciform structure was the inspiration for this beautiful miniature, from a twelfth-century book of sermons. The Ascension is framed within a section of the church, while the Twelve Apostles are ranged in a niche above.

century, doctrinal conflict had emerged once again. More profound and far-reaching in nature than before, it concerned the two contradictory natures of Christ, the human and the divine. The Orthodox view, propounded officially by the Council of Chalcedon in 451, accepted Christ's perfection both as God and as man. The heretical view, of which the Monophysites were the leading advocates, minimized Christ's human attributes and accepted only the concept of a single divinity that embraced Father, Son, and Holy Spirit in one. This Monophysite doctrine appealed in particular to the Oriental mind and temperament, and thus prevailed throughout Syria, Egypt, and the other eastern parts of the empire.

Justinian, as the personification of Orthodoxy, was tied both theologically and politically to the West; alliance with the pope was the basis of his imperial policy. But Theodora was an Oriental — and hence a Monophysite — who even aspired to convert the pope to her heretical beliefs when he visited Constantinople. Politically she looked not to the West but to the East. She had her own dream of empire, one in which she aspired, through religious toleration, to conciliate and strengthen the Byzantine Empire's eastern provinces — if necessary at the expense of a break with Rome. Failing to reconcile the two factions by peaceful means, Justinian came to persecute the very Monophysite heretics whom Theodora favored and was even known to harbor.

Still hoping to find a solution to the schism, the emperor involved himself increasingly in theological study and in the actual formulation of doctrine, thus trespassing on the ground of his own priesthood. In 553, he convened the fifth great council of the Church. Held in the secretariat of Hagia Sophia, it sought to appease the Monophysites through modifications in the Orthodox doctrine laid down at Chalcedon a century earlier, but the Orientals proved adamant in their refusal to accept any compromise. Their opposition was hardened by political mistrust of the central imperial government, and it was in this context that the emperor was bound, in his later treaty with the Persian king, to abstain from all religious propaganda in Persian territory. Thus Justinian died without achieving religious unity for the Byzantine Empire. Had the influence of Theodora prevailed, the empire — which faced both ways, like the double-headed eagle that later became its emblem — might well have achieved greater solidarity between East and West, and it might thus have resisted more easily the later successive encroachments of Persians, Arabs, and Turks.

Through the centuries, meanwhile, Hagia Sophia lived as the heart, pulse, and nerve center of Byzantine Christendom. The other churches of the empire ministered to their communities four times daily: at the First Hour, giving thanks for the light of the new day; at the Third, commemorating the descent of the Holy Spirit; at the Sixth (noon), commemorating the Crucifixion; and at the Ninth, commemorating the death of Christ. Apart from the various sacraments, prayers were said for a mother on the day her child was born and for the women who assisted at the birth. Others blessed a new house or a departure on a journey, especially by sea.

In the great church, however, services were held only on Sundays, on the days of the various saints,

Justinian, in military garb, appears on
both sides of a gold medallion (left)
commemorating a victory by his
general Belisarius over the Vandals.
In 540 Belisarius conquered Ravenna,
which quickly became the cultural
center of the Byzantine Empire in Italy.
At right are two exquisite mosaics from
the Church of San Vitale in Ravenna
portraying Justinian and his court
(above) and his wife, Theodora, and
her attendants (below).

apostles, and martyrs, and on other festivals of Church
and State. But these were numerous, ranging through
the cycle of the Annunciation, Nativity, Circumcision,
Epiphany, Holy Week, Ascension, Whitsuntide, Trans-
figuration, and Candlemas to such sacred festivals as
the raising of the Cross, events in the life of the Virgin
Mary, and the discovery of the True Cross. Such imperial festivals as the foundation of the city, coronations, and thanksgivings for victory in battle were also
celebrated in Hagia Sophia with a splendor prescribed
by tradition. This applied especially to the celebration
of the Divine Liturgy on the principal holy days of
the year, days when the emperor graced the church
with his presence.

The fixed order and procedure of this ritual was later
recorded in elaborate detail by the tenth-century emperor Constantine Porphyrogenitus, as a guide for
his son, the future Romanus II. Initiating each ritual
was an imperial procession to the church, an event
that the Lord High Chamberlains announced to the
emperor — and at his behest to the palace function-
aries — on the previous day. Orders were then issued
that, in preparation, the streets should be cleaned,
strewn with sawdust, and adorned with flowers. The
following morning the emperor emerged from his
private apartments clad in the *scaramangion* — a
caftan-like robe that was sometimes white and sometimes purple — and prayed before the image of Christ
in the oratory of the Golden Hall of his palace. Then,
robed by his chamberlains in a gold-hemmed, knee-
length cloak, he proceeded under their escort to say
prayers in the various shrines of the palace, ending in
the Church of Saint Stephen, where he prostrated him-

self three times before the great Cross of Constantine.
He was then clothed in the *chlamys,* a white imperial
mantle trimmed with gold, and invested with the
crown — which might, according to the occasion, be
white, red, or green. In the course of his procession to
the church there were six "receptions," during which
various imperial officials and commanders did the emperor reverence. These encounters took place in the
palace itself, before its brazen gate, on the square of
the Augustaeum, and finally at the entrance to the
vestibule of the narthex of Hagia Sophia. Having proceeded through the church, pausing for a series of
ritual ceremonies, the emperor entered the *metatorion,*
an enclosure occupying the east bay of the south aisle
that was reserved primarily for royalty and housed the
imperial throne. Here the emperor sat during the next
stage of the ceremony.

When the consecrated elements of bread and wine
were to be brought to the altar, the emperor, preceded by the scepters and banners, went behind the
ambo with his personal guard and the senators. There
the holy vessels and lighted lamps stood ready for him.
Lamp in hand, he proceeded to the solea, where, standing before the holy doors, he placed the lamp on the
balustrade. The elements of the mass were then carried
into the sanctuary, and the emperor bowed to the
patriarch and returned to the *metatorion.*

In the course of the ceremony he emerged twice
more. First, he came forward to bestow the Kiss of
Peace upon the patriarch, the imperial representative
of his council, the metropolitans, the archbishops, the
high priests of the great church, and the dignitaries
of the patriarchate — all of whom were led before him

MAXIMIANVS

The emperor on horseback in the central panel
of the imperial diptych at right — known as the
Barberini Ivory — is traditionally identified as
Justinian. The scene below shows barbarians
bearing tribute; above, two winged Victories
flank the figure of Christ. On the left is a military
consul; the matching panel is missing.

by the patriarchal ambassador. He then gave a Kiss
of Peace to the members of the senate, who were led
forward by the master of ceremonies, and retired once
more to the *metatorion*. He emerged a second time to
receive Holy Communion, a ceremony recounted in
particular detail by Constantine Porphyrogenitus in
relation to the Christmas liturgy. Accompanied by the
Lord High Chamberlains, the emperor approached
the patriarch, "for communion in the sacred Body and
Blood of Our Lord Jesus Christ." Two ostiaries, or
doorkeepers, held an unfolded cloth before him:

> Taking the precious gift in his hands, he kisses the
> Patriarch and, descending the steps and crossing him-
> self three times, he partakes of the holy bread. He
> ascends the steps once more, the ostiaries spread the
> holy cloth beneath him, and he receives the wine from
> the Patriarch. He steps down and prays. Emperor and
> Patriarch bow deeply to one another. Then the Em-
> peror returns into the *metatorion* and breakfasts with
> patricians and other dignitaries whom he has invited.

These were usually light repasts consisting of wine
mixed with water, and bread, cakes, or fruit — all
served in a section of the imperial enclosure reserved
for this purpose. After the meal the emperor once
again donned his *chlamys* and summoned the patriarch.
Together they went to the portico of the Holy Well,
whose marble verge was traditionally believed to be
the stone on which Christ sat when he talked with the
woman of Samaria. Nearby was the trumpet said to
have been used by Joshua to fell the walls of Jericho.
There the chancellor called up those chosen to receive
purses of gold — gifts customarily distributed at this
time to the archdeacon, the doorkeeper, other church
officers, the choristers, and the poor. These the emperor
doled out with his own hand. He was then crowned
once more by the patriarch, who anointed him with
sacred oil. After this he left the church and returned,
amid a series of official greetings and acclamations, to
his palace, where the attendants of his chamber wished
him "Many good New Years."

Such ceremonial surrounded a Byzantine prince
from the moment of his birth "in the purple" — within
the Purple Bedchamber of the Purple Palace, which
was faced with slabs of porphyry. When the emperor
had received in audience the congratulations of the
chief senators, the new-born prince was greeted with
his chosen name and his imperial parents were acclaimed by the people of the city in a ceremony at
the Hippodrome. Then he was taken to the entrance
of the church, to be clothed in white and named amid
Christian prayers. Meanwhile, in the tradition of the
Magi, ladies of rank brought presents to the empress
in token of her happy delivery. A deputation of dignitaries followed, bowing before the cradle and paying
their respects to the sovereign mother. A seven-day
period of public rejoicing ensued during which the
empress's health was drunk in a special spiced beverage.
It was only after a year had elapsed that the prince
was baptized at Hagia Sophia. After the ceremony he
was brought back to the palace through streets hung
with gold-embroidered silks. The emperor, clad in
purple, walked beside him, and the empress waited in
the palace to receive him.

Although acclaimed on his accession like a Roman
Caesar by the senate, the army, and the people of
Constantinople, a new emperor was not fully and visi-

The century-long ban on images that had led to the destruction of figural mosaics throughout Constantinople was finally resolved in 842 with the political defeat of the Iconoclasts. Among the major mosaics executed during the subsequent redecoration of Hagia Sophia was the late ninth-century lunette — of Leo VI prostrate at Christ's feet — over the Imperial Door in the narthex (left). The detail at right — of the richly robed Christ and the archangel Gabriel in a medallion — clearly indicates that technical knowledge and artistic inspiration had survived the lengthy prohibition.

bly invested with his rank until crowned by the patriarch. Such was the measure of the distinction between the old Roman and the new Christian empire. The emperor's divine mandate depended on the patriarch, who owed his appointment to God — and to the emperor only as God's instrument. The imperial oath, signifying both the emperor's tenure and his religious creed, was sworn "in Christ God faithful emperor and autocrat of the Romans," and submitted to "my most holy lord and ecumenical patriarch, lord . . . and with him to the divine and sacred synod."

Through the imperial centuries pilgrims from Russia and other countries thronged to Constantinople, and especially to the famed shrine of Hagia Sophia. The Russians owed their Christian beliefs largely to the missionary spirit of the city, where a school was established to educate missionaries bound for Slavic lands. The pilgrims absorbed, embellished, and spread throughout Christendom the innumerable legends concerning the great church recounted by its guardians. They were amazed by the richness of its treasures — by its gold and silver crosses and chalices "set with precious stones and pearls"; by its magnificent tombs of saints and martyrs (to say nothing of the iron bed, like a grill, on which at least one of them, Saint Lawrence, was said to have been roasted); and above all by the unparalleled store of sacred relics that comprised the church's renowned collection.

A portion of the True Cross was brought to the city of Constantine soon after the relic was discovered in A.D. 326. As time went by, additional fragments found their way to other parts of the world, but the main part of the Cross remained in Jerusalem until the city was

taken by the Persians in 614. Soon the armies of Khosrau II were threatening Constantinople, and the Emperor Heraclius was only dissuaded from abandoning the city and transferring his capital to Carthage by the action of the patriarch, who bound him not to do so by an oath solemnly administered in Hagia Sophia.

Heraclius eventually defeated the Persians and brought the Cross back to Constantinople. After reposing for a while in Hagia Sophia, it was returned briefly to Jerusalem before being removed again. This time four parts of it remained behind. Of the fifteen other parts, Constantinople retained three in addition to that of Saint Helena, which was lodged in a reliquary in Hagia Sophia. These were made into a cross with two arms, and each year at the Feast of the Adoration of the Holy Cross this "Holy Wood" was elevated and worshiped in the sanctuary by both emperor and patriarch.

According to an anonymous chronicler, the Cross "works healing wonders, and drives away diseases and demons." He adds that in every column of the church, both above and below, "is placed one sacred relic." Robert of Clari, a French knight of the thirteenth century, declared that each of Hagia Sophia's columns had "a medicinal quality; some keep off *mal des reins,* some *mal du flanc,* and other diseases." Indeed, miraculous properties were attributed to some of the columns, notably a "sweating column" in the northwest corner of the church that exuded moisture through holes in the stone. Anthony, Archbishop of Novgorod, connected the column with Saint Gregory Thaumaturgus, "the worker of Miracles." According to the Russian

prelate, the column was "encased in plates of brass; and beside this column Saint Gregory once appeared, wherefore the people now kiss it, rubbing against it their chests and shoulders to cure them of their ills." He adds that on the saint's feast day his relics were brought to the column. The Byzantines as well as the Turks saw it as a panacea for diseases of the eye. The amount of healing moisture available depended upon the faith of the sufferer, however, and for some the stone remained dry.

Similarly, a miraculous oil was said to flow from certain holy relics; on one occasion, the salve was reported to have healed Justinian himself. There were also miracle-working icons, among them a mosaic of Christ to which another Russian, Stephen of Novgorod, refers. According to his accounts, holy water flowed from the wounds on this Christ's feet. The sacred Mandelion, an icon known as the "Christ not painted by human hands" that was captured in battle in the tenth century and brought to the great church in a ceremonial procession, had also been installed in Hagia Sophia.

In the eighth and ninth centuries the Byzantine Empire was torn by a strong and often turbulent reaction against the worship of all such icons and sacred relics. This was the Iconoclast controversy. Launched through the proscription of images by the Emperor Leo III in 726, it ebbed and flowed for nine decades before being resolved in 843 by a council whose decisions — representing a triumph for Orthodoxy — are still celebrated by an annual festival of the Greek Orthodox Church.

This prolonged dispute represented a further stage in the perennial theological conflict between East and West, for during the eighth century the cult of images came to be seen as a form of idolatry. It flourished not only in the churches of the cities but in the monasteries, whose growing wealth and influence were a source of concern to the State. Superstition was increasing; the mass of worshipers, many of them iconodules, tended to see icons — particularly those with miraculous properties — not simply as sacred pictures but as mystical personifications of Christ, the Virgin, or one of the saints, and to venerate them as such.

The reaction against the cult of images coincided with a period of Arab invasions of the Byzantine Empire, and was indeed comparable to the Islamic prohibition of all human images. The Arab campaign of 717 culminated in a siege of Constantinople that was repelled by Leo III, called the Isaurian, thus saving the empire. On this occasion there was no exhorting of the miraculous icon of the Virgin, as there had been during the first Persian siege a century earlier. For Leo was an Asian and a man of Iconoclast sympathies. He had relied for his empire's defense against the Arabs not upon miracles but upon the ascetic peasant soldiery of Asia Minor, many of whom ascribed previous defeats of the Christians to an increase of corruption and idolatry within their Church. Hence Leo's reformist decree. Initially moderate in intent, it led, as time went by, to persecutions, the widespread destruction of works of church art, and the dissolution or secularization of monasteries.

Leo personally destroyed a figure of Christ over the gate of his palace in Constantinople and it was later replaced with a large cross and an inscription: "The

The Iconoclasts were literally "image-breakers,"
as can be seen in the manuscript illustration at left
in which an image of Christ is being obliterated
with whitewash. Only abstract decorations, such as
the mosaic tiles that surround a window in *Hagia
Sophia* (below), escaped the Iconoclasts' wrath.

emperor cannot endure that Christ should be represented by a mute and lifeless image graven of earthly materials. But Leo and his young son Constantine have at their gates engraved the thrice-blessed representation of the cross, the glory of believing monarchs." As emperor, the son was to prove even more extreme than his father, condemning not only images but all adoration of the Virgin and intercession of the saints. Constantine V decreed that "there shall be rejected, removed, and cursed, out of the Christian Church, every likeness which is made out of any material whatever by the evil art of painters" — a decree that led to further orgies of destruction. And when, in 742, the pretender Artavasdus was crowned by an iconodule patriarch in Hagia Sophia, he and his sons were ejected and blinded by the emperor, while the patriarch endured the public humiliation of a ride around the Hippodrome on the back of a donkey.

The disgraced patriarch's successor is said to have destroyed "the images of gold mosaic and wax encaustic" in the churches of Constantinople. His ravages were so thorough that the last of the Iconoclast emperors, Theophilus, was pleased to observe that, "throughout every church the figures of the saints were destroyed, and the forms of beasts and birds were painted in their places." But after the death of Theophilus, during the regency of his widow, Theodora, the ban on images was finally raised. Their restoration, in 842, was made on condition that "the worship due to God and the veneration due to created things were carefully observed."

The extent to which Hagia Sophia itself may have suffered in the course of this conflict is uncertain; there

57

The tenth-century mosaic lunette over the south door in the vestibule of Hagia Sophia (below) is a magnificent blend of religious and political themes. As protector of Church and State, the enthroned Madonna accepts a model of the city of Constantinople from Constantine and a model of Hagia Sophia from Justinian (detail at right).

was undoubtedly some destruction of its images, but others were saved. We know only that "the victory of the image-worshipers was celebrated by the installation of the long-banished pictures in Saint Sophia on the 19th February 842, just thirty days after the death of Theophilus."

In the time of Justinian there were certainly portraits of Christ, the Virgin, angels, prophets, and apostles on the chancel screen, and his successor, Justin II, introduced some mosaics, including portraits of saints that the Iconoclasts removed and replaced with crosses. But the mosaic decoration of the church itself seems to have been largely if not wholly nonfigural, hence immune to the attacks of image-breakers. Its dome was of pure gold mosaic, with a mosaic cross in the center. Other mosaics, executed in silver, red, blue, and green on a background of gold, were abstract designs not of figures but of crosses, stars, squares, roundels, swastikas, and floral and vegetal scrolls.

At that time mosaics were made by setting small cubes of glass in moist plaster. Gold or silver leaf was applied to the exposed surface, which was then coated with a protective layer of glaze. It was not until the ninth century, after the end of the iconoclastic era, that the use of natural stones and terracotta, in addition to glass, was introduced, a technique that led to a new phase in the art of mosaic.

The redecoration of Hagia Sophia began in the late ninth century, at the same time the second Golden Age of the Byzantine Empire began. In view of its size and its architectural complexity, the great church was less suited to figural mosaic treatment than other, smaller domed cruciform churches of this time,

As the political and spiritual center of the Byzantine Empire, Constantinople benefited from imperial patronage. The greatest artistic skill was lavished on the decoration of the city's churches — particularly Hagia Sophia. The anonymous ninth-century artists responsible for the huge mosaic of the Virgin and Child in the bema of the apse (far left) created an image of astonishing grandeur and tenderness. The vibrant palette of the tiles accentuates the serene beauty of the simply garbed Virgin. So lifelike is the portrayal that she appears about to rise from her cushioned throne. Two standing archangels originally flanked the Virgin in the bema but only fragments remain of the figure of Michael. At left is a close-up of the ethereal and tranquil face of the surviving panel, that of the archangel Gabriel. Below is an eleventh-century mosaic from the south gallery of the church showing Christ Pantocrator between the Empress Zoë and her third husband, Constantine IX Monomachus. The stiffly posed and elaborately costumed monarchs proffer symbolic donations — a purse of silver and a bull of privileges.

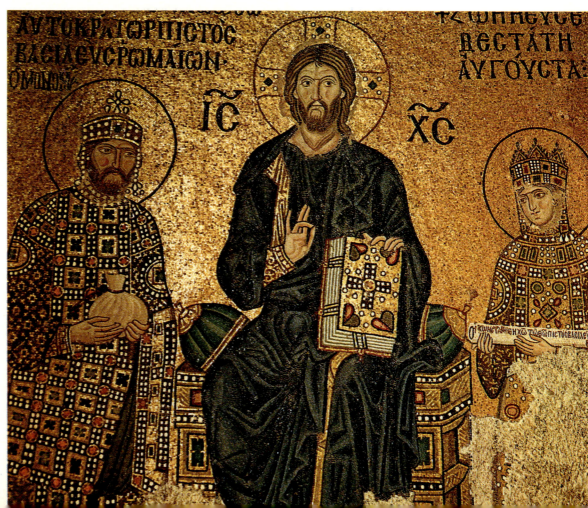

whose interiors could be seen at a glance and hence treated as a unit in decorative terms. Hagia Sophia's walls, on the other hand, are sheathed in marble and broken by colonnades. They rise to a height of seventy-five feet from the floor of the nave, and because so much of the structure is intricately jointed and curved, little wall space is available for figural mosaics. To be in scale when seen from below, such figures would have to be three times life-size. On the flat wall surfaces in the niches of the tympana, the space allowed for figures is a mere six feet high; hence the mosaics set into those niches are virtually invisible from the level of the nave. In addition, the great width of the nave disrupts any relationship between the figure groups featured on opposite, lateral walls.

Thus in its overall architectural design, the interior of the church — with its aisles and galleries half out of sight of the nave — is not seen as a whole and does not lend itself to any unified scheme of figural decoration. For this reason the figural mosaics of Hagia Sophia that illuminated the church from the ninth century onward presented not a cohesive, scintillant Christian universe in narrative terms — as do the mosaics in such smaller churches as the fourteenth-century Saint Saviour in Chora (the Kariye Camii) — but a series of separate sacred tableaux. These occupied, successively, the dome, the pendentives, the apse, the arches, the tympana, the bays of the galleries, and the lunettes above the principal doors.

In the center of the dome, brooding gravely over the church, was a great mosaic figure of Christ Pantocrator — Christ as God. The figure was twice destroyed, and it is unlikely that any of the original cubes survive be-

The seemingly limitless wall space within Hagia Sophia provided a rich field for virtuoso craftsmanship. In the view at left, abstract mosaics adorn the arches above the massive pillars.

neath the present coating of plaster and Koranic inscription. Four six-winged seraphs filled the four pendentives. Today two of them are reproduced on a coating of plaster, while the other two survive in mosaic form. Their faces, once set with a "stern expression calling to mind the ancient renderings of the head of Medusa," are concealed beneath gilded stars.

But in the half dome of the apse, the Virgin and Child survive intact. Robed in blue, she sits on a jeweled throne, serene and spiritual, yet human, the Child on her knee robed in gold. The figure is actually sixteen feet high, but looks small from the nave. In the arches on either side were two attendant archangels: Michael, who has vanished but for the tips of his wings; and Gabriel, who survives, his elongated face paler than the Virgin's — to suggest his unearthly nature — but his dress and demeanor both nobly imperial. Rich garlands complete the adornment of the apse, celebrating the artistic as well as theological triumph of Orthodoxy over iconoclasm.

Following tradition, the great eastern and western arches were originally occupied by mosaics of the apostles. Fragments of Peter and Paul, flanking a medallion of the Virgin and Child, were uncovered here in the nineteenth century, only to be destroyed at a later date. During the same period a figure of Saint John the Baptist was briefly uncovered before being recoated with plaster, as was an image of the standing Virgin. The plasterers also covered a symbol of the divine presence in the form of a throne with a book of the Gospels upon it, a triple cross above it with a Crown of Thorns, and a mosaic portrait of Emperor John V Palaeologus. In the tympana, standing in rows beneath two pairs of angels, were four major and twelve minor prophets, all of whom have vanished, and fourteen bishops in hieratic poses and vestments, three of whom have survived.

Portraits of emperors were an integral feature in the mosaic decoration of Hagia Sophia. Anthony of Novgorod, writing during the first decade of the thirteenth century, claimed to have seen likenesses of all the patriarchs of Constantinople and all the Byzantine emperors on the walls of the church. Mosaics symbolizing Heaven and Earth, Church and State, the spiritual and the secular, greeted the worshiper as he entered the great church — and all of these survive to greet the twentieth-century visitor as he enters the echoing nave of Hagia Sophia today.

Filling the lunette above the southern entrance is an offertory group in whose center is the enthroned Virgin Mary, the "Queen of Heaven," with the Child on her lap. Two crowned emperors stand beside her: Constantine on her left, proffering a model of his fortress-city of Constantinople, of which she is guardian; Justinian on her right, proffering a model of Hagia Sophia, of which she is patron. This mosaic, which dates from the late tenth century, was executed more than a century after the symbolic group that hovers over the door from the narthex into the nave. There, on a jeweled, cushioned, lyre-backed throne, sits a majestic figure of Christ, twice life-size, his right hand raised in blessing and his left holding an open book inscribed, "Peace be with you, I am the Light of the World." Flanking him are two medallions, one of the Virgin Mary with her hands extended in prayer, the other of an angel with a wand in its hand. Prostrated at Christ's feet is the

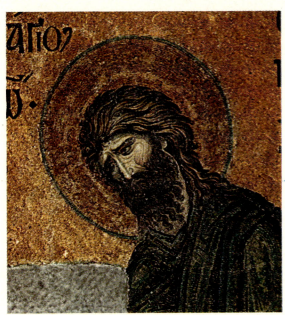

The thirteenth-century Deesis in the south gallery of Hagia Sophia is a triumph of the mosaicist's art. An astonishingly lifelike portrayal of Christ (right) appears between the sensitively modeled figures of the Virgin (far left) and Saint John the Baptist (near left).

submissive figure of an emperor — either Basil I or his son Leo VI of the Macedonian dynasty — clad in a purple robe and extending both hands in a gesture of supplication to his celestial lord, who represents the human embodiment of the Holy Wisdom from which Hagia Sophia takes its name.

An early tenth-century imperial portrait, recently uncovered on the face of a pier in the north gallery, shows the "Orthodox and faithful Emperor Alexander" as a youth with a ruddy complexion and a short brown beard. Another son of Basil I, Alexander was a lover of sport who reigned as sole emperor for little more than a year before collapsing and dying after a hard game of polo.

In the south gallery, flanking an enthroned figure of Christ, are the eleventh-century emperor Constantine IX Monomachus, and his empress Zoë. This grouping illustrates a number of changes in mosaic technique, among them the use of smaller cubes set in bands that follow the contours of face and bones, giving the figures a more realistic aspect. Zoë had three successive imperial husbands, and study of the mosaic suggests that the portrait was originally that of her first husband, Romanus III, whose inscribed name and features were later exchanged for those of her third husband, Constantine IX.

The last of this series of imperial portrait groups features John II Comnenus, who reigned through the first half of the twelfth century. A grave, finely drawn figure, he is shown standing to the right of the Virgin and Child. To the Virgin's left stands the emperor's consort, Irene, her face made up like a mask and her blond hair elaborately plaited according to the fashion of the time. Their young son Alexius stands beyond her on a projecting pilaster, his mournful features marked by an incipient moustache.

Wholly spiritual in its essence — and hence different in character from these imperial portraits — is the large mosaic group of the Deesis, a devotional composition, familiar throughout the Byzantine Empire, that commonly framed the central group of the Last Judgment. In Hagia Sophia it occupies the middle bay of the south gallery. Its theme is traditional: Saint John the Baptist, the last prophet of the old dispensation, and the Virgin Mary, embodiment of the new, interceding with Christ on behalf of humanity. Much of the mosaic has vanished, but the three principal figures survive, and they are studies in refinement and pathos. Christ, enthroned in the center, is for all his majesty the embodiment of Christian love and compassion. The Baptist reclines before him with humble devotion; the Virgin, with tender serenity. A spirit of humanity lights up their sorrowful features, portrayed with a subtlety rarely achieved in mosaic. Fragments of an earlier Deesis have also survived, along with several other mosaic figures, in an unused, vaulted chamber off the southern end of the great church's west gallery.

The great Deesis in the south gallery dates from the latter part of the thirteenth century. As such it is the latest of all the mosaics in Hagia Sophia — and also the finest. It is the product of a humanist renaissance that came to full flower only during the last two centuries of the Byzantine Empire's existence. In the interim, however, a major catastrophe had befallen the empire, the city of Constantinople, and the great church of Hagia Sophia alike.

IV
Under Alien Rule

The "God-guarded city" of Constantinople withstood no fewer than seventeen sieges between the time it was founded in 330 and the end of the twelfth century. Protected not only by the sacred image of the Virgin Mary but by the impregnable land walls of Emperor Theodosius II, it repelled the successive invasions of barbarians, Avars, Bulgars, Arabs, and Russians. Then, at the start of the thirteenth century, the city finally fell — not to an attack from the land but from the sea, and not to the infidel but to a Christian army. It was the Christian powers of Western Europe that first occupied and sacked Constantinople, fatally disrupting the Byzantine Empire, weakening it against later invasions from the Islamic East, and inflicting upon it a blow from which it was not, in the long run, to recover.

The perennial religious strife between East and West, between the Orthodox and the Roman Catholic doctrines, had been exacerbated in the West by the Iconoclast controversy. This aroused widespread resistance from the monastic orders in Europe, led to the loss of Ravenna and much of southern Italy, and created a breach between the Byzantine Empire and the papacy — prompting the pope to seek new allies among the Frankish powers of the Latin West. The results of this move were to be far-reaching: on Christmas Day 800, the pope crowned Charlemagne Holy Roman Emperor, reviving the Roman Empire of the West under an "heir of the Caesars" with claims of supremacy in Christendom at the expense of the Eastern Empire's authority. Conflict, both religious and political, was henceforth intensified between Rome and Constantinople.

Meanwhile, the fortunes of the Byzantine Empire rose and fell. Under the Macedonian dynasty that flourished from 867 until the mid-eleventh century, the empire regained much of its former strength and authority. Basil I and his successors recaptured the lost provinces in southern Italy, and throughout the tenth century they restored Byzantine prestige in the Mediterranean, consolidating a revived protectorate of "Magna Graecia" on Italian shores. They held their own against the German kings who aspired, as Holy Roman emperors, to establish their sway in these parts. At the cost of substantial commercial privileges, they allied themselves securely with the maritime republic of Venice, which helped them maintain their prestige in the Adriatic.

But in the eleventh century the empire entered a period of decline. The Macedonian dynasty petered out with a series of weak rulers; in the West the Normans, a new aggressive power backed by the papacy, invaded southern Italy and soon wrested from the Byzantine Empire all its Italian possessions. They landed on the coast of Epirus and attempted to gain control over the coast of the Adriatic with an attack on Durazzo. Their invasion force was driven off by the Venetians, however, and Norman aggression was temporarily checked.

Meanwhile, in 1054, religious conflict between East and West had reached a climax with the final and irreparable schism between the Roman and Orthodox churches. The Patriarch of Constantinople, Michael Cerularius, goaded by the presumption and arrogance of Pope Leo IX, accused the pontiff of heresy. The pope retorted in kind. "The rising majesty of Rome,"

Gibbon observed, "could no longer brook the insolence of a rebel; and Michael Ccrularius was excommunicated in the heart of Constantinople by the Pope's legates." An anathema enumerating seven Greek heresies was placed on the altar of Hagia Sophia, but the Greeks would not recant their errors. Successive popes would not repeal the sentence, and thus, as Gibbon notes, "from this thunderbolt we may date the consummation of the schism."

Meanwhile, the perennial military conflict proceeded on two fronts. The loss of Italy to the Normans in the West coincided with the first invasion of the empire by the Seljuk Turks from the East. Crossing the Byzantine frontier in 1071 to fight the battle of Manzikert, the Turks soon controlled most of Asia Minor. Their invasion led to direct retaliation in the form of the Crusades, a series of holy wars launched by the West in the eleventh and twelfth centuries in order to liberate Jerusalem and its shrines of Christian pilgrimage. But far from uniting the eastern and western arms of Christendom against the infidel, the Crusades only intensified their mutual antagonism.

The armies of the First Crusade, destined to capture Jerusalem with the aid of a strong contingent of Normans, arrived before the gates of Constantinople in 1098. Their arrival coincided with a period of Byzantine revival under the brilliant dynasty of the Comnenes. Emperor Alexius I, although perturbed at the intrusion, received the crusading barons diplomatically. Indeed, he sought to turn the Crusade to his own account, to recover his lost Asian provinces. But his hopes were dashed, for when the Normans under Bohemund succeeded in recapturing Antioch,

they usurped it as a principality of their own. Other Latin princes did likewise in Syria, disregarding their initial oath of allegiance to the emperor, and recriminations on both sides grew bitter. The Latin kingdom of Jerusalem was from the outset divided among four rival baronies and numerous minor fiefs. Internal discord grew, and from the middle of the eleventh century the kingdom fell into a decline.

The failure of the Second Crusade (1147–49), which sought to recapture Jerusalem, was blamed by the Latins on the perfidy of the Greeks. The Third Crusade also failed to recapture the Holy City, and there was talk in the West of a Crusade of revenge against the Byzantine Empire itself. Each campaign further widened the abyss between Greek and Latin Christians.

Although envenomed by theological schisms, this conflict was basically a political and social feud between peoples at two differing stages of civilization. The Greeks of the East saw the Latins of the West as impious barbarians — an uncouth, undisciplined breed deficient in culture and refinement, insolent in manners, predatory, and so greedy for gain that, as the imperial historian Anna Comnena wrote of them, they would "sell for an obol even what they held most dear" — even their wives and children. Gibbon also noted this combination of cupidity and crudity:

Of this hostile temper a large portion may doubtless be ascribed to the difference of language, dress, and manners, which severs and alienates the nations of the globe. The pride, as well as the prudence, of the sovereign was deeply wounded by the intrusion of foreign armies, that claimed a right of traversing his

Beset by enemies during the eleventh century, the Byzantine emperors struggled to maintain control over their far-flung empire. The miniatures below, from the famous Skylitzes manuscript, depict two of the recurrent clashes with the Arabs. With the accession of Alexius I Comnenus in 1081, the Arab threat was temporarily quelled but Alexius (portrayed at right beside the seated figure of Christ) soon faced a greater threat from the Franks.

dominions and pressing under the walls of his capital; his subjects were insulted and plundered by the rude strangers of the West; and the hatred of the pusillanimous Greeks was sharpened by secret envy of the bold and pious enterprises of the Franks.

The conflict reached its disastrous climax with the Fourth Crusade, which was launched at the outset of the thirteenth century. This precipitated the decline and fall of the Eastern Empire, which owed as much to Byzantine decadence as to Frankish enterprise. As the Comnene dynasty lapsed into weakness and disunity, Venice changed sides and supported the Normans, who advanced through the Balkans to capture and sack Salonika. The Greeks had given the Normans ample pretext for such punitive action: the invasion followed a xenophobic outburst in Constantinople that had resulted in the brutal massacre of Frankish merchants and other Latin Christians.

Andronicus I, who inspired the outburst, was himself overthrown two years later, to be succeeded by Isaac II, founder of the worthless but short-lived Angelus dynasty. The first of a pair of emperors who were known as the "Earthly Angels," he was a man who, in Gibbon's words, "slept on the throne, and was awakened only by the sounds of pleasure." In 1195 Isaac was dethroned and blinded by his brother, Alexius III, while his young son fled from prison into exile. "The scruples of the first Crusaders," as Gibbon saw it, "had neglected the fairest opportunities of securing, by the possession of Constantinople, the way to the Holy Land; a domestic revolution invited and almost compelled the French and Venetians to achieve the conquest of the Roman Empire of the East."

A sacred mission — the reconquest of Jerusalem from the infidel — drew huge armies of Crusaders to the East in the eleventh and twelfth centuries. In 1204 the tempting prize of Constantinople, the richest city in Christendom, deflected the soldiers of the Fourth Crusade from their original objective — and their subsequent behavior belied the humble piety of the armored knight below.

The armies of the Fourth Crusade assembled in Venice as the twelfth century drew to a close. Their intended objective was Egypt and the Holy Land. For transport they depended by agreement on the ships of the Venetians, upon whose naval and mercantile predominance the Eastern Empire itself had until lately relied. When the knights ran short of funds with which to keep to their bargain, the Venetians craftily turned the Crusade to their own mercenary ends. They persuaded the knights first to recapture for Venice the Christian port of Zara, which had fallen into the hands of the Hungarians, and then to divert the main Crusade, en route to Egypt and the Holy Land, to the Christian city of Constantinople.

The political pretext for such a diversion was the installation of Isaac's exiled son, the pretender Alexius, on the throne of his uncle Alexius III. Upon his accession he promised not only to finance the expedition and to reinforce it with arms, but to submit the Church of Constantinople to Rome. Crusading conscience could in part be eased by reflecting that Constantinople was itself a Holy City and a center of pilgrimage — the New Jerusalem, rich in the sacred relics of the old, which should be freed from the illicit possession of the "godless" Greeks.

Thus, in the summer of 1203, the Venetian fleet with its cargo of crusading Franks appeared before the walls of Constantinople and landed near Galata on the Golden Horn. The Franks gazed in covetous expectation across to the legendary city, which they knew by repute as the wealthiest on earth — a city "sovereign over all others," containing two-thirds of the world's riches. Encouraged by the young Alexius to expect no

70

resistance, the Crusaders were disconcerted to find the gates closed against them. But the seawalls proved less strong than the land walls, and after an initial repulse the Venetians effected a breach.

Upon receiving the news that Emperor Alexius III had fled and his blind brother Isaac had been restored to the throne, they desisted from further attacks, halting their armies on the opposite shore. At their insistence, young Alexius was raised as coemperor with his father. He was crowned Alexius IV in Hagia Sophia on Saint Peter's Day, "full worthily and with honor according to the use of the Greek Emperors at that time," according to Geoffroy de Villehardouin, the Crusades' historian. But the young Alexius — "this baby," as his superiors contemptuously called him — soon found that the imperial funds were insufficient to meet the extortionate demands of the Venetians. Therefore, in addition to raising new and unpopular taxes he seized large quantities of plate from Hagia Sophia, melted down its golden lamps and silver candelabra, stripped the iconostasis of its plating, and requisitioned jeweled icons and reliquaries from other churches throughout the city.

The clergy, who had sullenly refused to accept Roman supremacy and Latin usages, were thus further enraged. The populace fiercely resented the spectacle of the Frankish knights striding haughtily through the streets and gazing with a mixture of wonder, contempt, and greed upon the first really civilized city they had ever seen. Unable to comprehend the enlightened self-interest that had prompted the Byzantines to maintain polite relations with their infidel neighbors, a gang of pious Frenchmen burned down the mosque used by visiting Moslem merchants. The consequent fire raged through the city for eight days and nights, cutting a swath three miles wide through the heart of Constantinople and endangering Hagia Sophia itself. "It is not easy," Gibbon wrote, "to count the stately churches and palaces that were reduced to a smoking ruin, to value the merchandise that perished in the trading streets, or to number the families that were involved in the common destruction."

As indignation mounted on both sides, a delegation of Crusaders confronted Alexius IV with a demand for the fulfillment of his promises. As they left the palace empty-handed, the delegates were set upon by an angry mob, which then stormed into the great church and demanded the deposition of Alexius. "A great crowd gathered together in Santa Sophia," wrote the thirteenth-century Byzantine historian Nicetas Acominatus, "the whole Senate and the high dignitaries of the Church. But when we had collected their votes, no conclusion could be reached as to who should be made Emperor if Alexius was deposed." After three days of indecisive debate, the choice of the parties fell on an obscure and reluctant nobleman, Nicolas Canobus, who chanced to be present. At this the son-in-law of Alexius IV, Alexius Ducas — familiarly known as Mourtzuphlos because of his bushy eyebrows, which met in the middle — seized the imperial throne. He was crowned in Hagia Sophia as Alexius V, which led Villehardouin to exclaim, "Now see if ever people were guilty of such humble treachery." For meanwhile Alexius IV had been thrown into a dungeon and strangled. His father, Isaac, died from a combination of grief and fright a few days later.

Sachiez que .M. C. et quatreuinz ans ap[re]s lincarnation n[ost]re sengnor ie such[ri]st al tens Innocent apostoille de Rome et phelippe Roy de france. et Richart Roy dengleterre et un saint home en france qui ot nom folques de nuilli. Cil nuillis si est entre ligui sor marne e paris. et il ere p[re]stres et tenoit la parroiche de la uille. Et cil folques dont ie uos di comenca a parler de dieu par france et par les autres terres entor. et n[ost]re sires fist maintes miracles por lui. Sachiez que la renomee de cel saint home ala tant que ele uint a lapostoille de Rome Innocent. et la postoille enuoia en france et manda al p[ro]dome quil preeschast deseuoiz par sautorite. et ap[re]s enuoia un sien chardonal maistre perron de chappes auiste. et il manda par lui le pardon tel o ie uos dirai. Tuit cil qui se auisseroient et seruoient le seruise deu un an en lost seroient quites de toz les pechiez que il auoient faiz dont il se seroient confes. Por ce q[ue] cil pardons fu issi g[ra]nz. si sen esmurent mult li cuers des gens. et mult sen auiserent porce q[ue] li pardon ere si g[ra]nz.

En lautre an ap[re]s q[ue] cil p[re]udon folques parla ensi de dieu ot un tornoi en la campaigne a un chastel qui ot nom aicis. Et par la grace de dieu si auint que tibaut quens de campaigne et de brie prist la croiz. et li quens loeys de blois et de chartein et ce fu a lentree des auens. Or sachiez que cil quens Thibauz ere iones hom. et nauoit pas plus de .xxii. anz. Ne si quens loeys nauoit pas plus de .xxvii. anz. Cil dui comte erent nouou le Roy de france q[ui] si cousin germain et neuou le Roi dengleterre de lautre part.

Auec ces .ii. contes se auiserent .ii. mult halt baron de france. Symons de monfort q[ue] Renauz de momiral. mult fu grant la renomee par les terres quant al .ii. halt home sen auiserent.

En la terre le conte Thibaut de campaigne se auisa garniers li euesques de troies. li quens Garniers de briene. Joffroi de Joenuile qui ere seneschaus de la terre. Robert ses freres. Gautiers de Gaignoru. Gautiers de mombeliart. Eustaches de chonelans. Gius de plaissie. ses freres. henris darsilleres. Ogiers de sain cheron. uilains de nuilli. Joffroi de uilehardoin. li mareschaus de campaigne. Joffroi ses niers. Guillelmes de nuilli. Gautiers de sullineres. Quus de monteingni. m[...]. Manassiers de lisle. Machaires

At left is a page from the original manuscript of The Chronicles of the Crusades, *an eyewitness account by Geoffroy de Villehardouin, a French nobleman who served in the Fourth Crusade. The illustration beneath the text depicts the beleaguered Byzantines attempting to defend their city against the Crusaders' attacks from land and sea.*

The Crusaders' response to this challenge was a major assault designed to capture the city and install a Latin emperor of their choice. Breaching the land walls, they overcame the defenders, many of whom were trapped by a second disastrous fire, and poured into the city. Alexius V fled, only to be captured by the Latins and flung to his death from the top of the Theodosian Column. On April 12, 1204, the nobles met in Hagia Sophia to offer the crown to Alexius's brother-in-law, Theodore Lascaris. Realizing that the city was lost, he refused the empty honor and emerged from the church with the patriarch. Outside in the square he harangued the Varangian Guard, traditionally loyal to the emperor, hoping to spur them to a last resistance. But his hope was vain. That night Theodore, his wife, the patriarch, and a party of noblemen slipped down to the harbor and sailed across the Bosporus to Asia. Constantinople had been conquered — by a Crusade against the Cross.

Enrico Dandolo, the blind doge of Venice, and the leading Crusaders promptly installed themselves in the abandoned imperial palace and authorized the soldiery to spend the next three days in pillage. According to British historian Sir Steven Runciman, the ensuing sack of Constantinople was one without parallel in all of human history:

> For nine centuries the great city had been the capital of Christian civilization. It was filled with works of art that had survived from ancient Greece and with the masterpieces of its own exquisite craftsmen. The Venetians indeed knew the value of such things. Wherever they could they seized treasures and carried them off to adorn the squares and churches and palaces of their town. But the Frenchmen and Flemings were filled with a lust for destruction. They rushed in a howling mob down the streets and through the houses, snatching up everything that glittered and destroying whatever they could not carry, pausing only to murder or to rape, or to break open the wine-cellars for their refreshment.

For three days the ghastly pillage and bloodshed continued: monasteries, churches, and libraries were looted and wrecked; nuns were ravished in their convents; and wounded women and children were left to die in the streets. When it was over, "the huge and beautiful city was a shambles."

In his *Chronicles of the Crusades,* one of the oldest surviving works of French prose, Villehardouin declares that never "since the creation of the world" had so much plunder been won in any city. It was "so great that none could tell you the end of it; gold and silver, and vessels and precious stones, and samite, and cloth of silk, and robes in vair and grey, and ermine, and every choicest thing found upon the earth." Such treasures were, as Gibbon assessed them, "the most precious, as they could not be procured for money in the ruder countries of Europe."

A century earlier Alexius I, founder of the Comnene dynasty, had written to Robert Count of Flanders, begging for Western assistance against the Turks, enumerating the holy relics scattered through the city, and adding: "If you do not care to fight for these, and gold will tempt you more, you will find more of it at Constantinople than in the whole world, for the treasures of its basilicas alone would be sufficient to furnish all the churches of Christendom, and all these

When the victorious soldiers of the Fourth Crusade entered
Constantinople in 1204, they were dazzled and overwhelmed by
the sheer wealth of the city. In an unprecedented and violent
rampage, they proceeded to strip the churches and public
buildings of their priceless treasures. According to
Villehardouin, "the booty gained was so great that none could
tell you the end of it . . . never, since the world was created,
had so much booty been won in any city." As financiers of the
Crusade, the Venetians claimed the largest portion of the loot.
The Treasury of Saint Mark's Cathedral in Venice now houses
the tenth-century gold and enamel book cover at left, adorned
with the winged figure of the archangel Michael; the lustrous
eleventh-century alabaster paten above, with an enamel of
Christ in the center and a jeweled rim; and the finely wrought
chalice at right. Made of sardonyx and silver gilt, adorned
with pearls and enameled medallions, the chalice is one of
thirty-two that were taken to Venice during the sack of
Constantinople. Among other incomparable products of
Byzantine craftsmanship now scattered about Europe is the
ninth-century reliquary known as the Beresford Hope Cross.
At upper left is the back of the enamel and gold cross, which
is mounted in silver gilt. In the center is the Virgin with her
arms outstretched, with busts of saints Peter, Andrew,
John the Baptist, and Paul around her.

treasures cannot together amount to those of Santa Sophia, whose riches have never been equalled."

So the Franks and the Venetians now saw for themselves. The Latin soldiers stormed into Hagia Sophia, drank out of chalices from which they had pried the precious stones, and set a prostitute to dancing before the altar. Ambo, iconostasis, doors, frames of icons, sacred vessels, reliquaries, crosses, and candlesticks were all stripped of their precious metals, which were melted down to be made into coin. Objects that proved to be made of copper gilt, not of gold, were destroyed in a rage by the plunderers. The Holy Table — or what remained of it — was shipped to Venice. En route, the vessel transporting it sank in the depths of the Propontis, where, a later chronicler records, "in time of calm, the sailors, pouring oil upon the waves, declare that they can see it gleaming in the abyss."

Nicetas, the Byzantine historian who chronicled the fall of Constantinople, lamented: "O city, city, the eye of all cities, famous through all the lands of the world, a monument of this world, mother of Churches, leader of faith, guide in Orthodoxy, nurse of learning, why have you had to drink this cup of fury from the Lord?" When the prescribed period of looting was over, the knights and the Venetians settled down to a systematic division of the rest of the spoils. These were collected together in three churches. "Then," Villehardouin writes, "each began to bring in such booty as he had taken, and to collect it together. And some brought in loyally, and some in evil sort, because covetousness, which is the root of all evil, let and hindered them. So from that time forth the covetous

began to keep things back and our Lord began to love them less." He adds that stern justice was meted out to those found guilty of theft, "and not a few were hanged." The Count of Saint Paul, for example, hanged one of his knights for failing to declare certain spoils. But many others were as guilty, so the exact extent of the booty could never be measured.

The bulk of the treasure was divided according to covenant: three-eighths for the Crusaders, three-eighths for the Venetians, and a quarter for the Latin emperor, who had yet to be chosen. Gibbon estimates that the French knights' share, after payment of their debts to the Venetians, amounted to seven times the annual revenue of England at the time. Much of the plunder was distributed in the form of hard gold and silver. For the purpose of base coinage, this was later supplemented by melting down a number of bronze classical statues: the Hera of Samos from Constantine's Forum, the Hercules of Lysippus from the Hippodrome, and others equally famous.

Over the next few years the city was almost denuded of Christian relics, many of them from Hagia Sophia, which found their way to all parts of the West. Soissons received the Veil of the Virgin, the heads of Saint John the Baptist and Saint Stephen, and the finger that Saint Thomas inserted into the side of Christ; Amiens received a head also thought to be that of the Baptist; Chartres, thanks to Louis of Blois, received the head of Saint Anne; Pisa, that of Saint John Chrysostom; Cologne, that of Saint Pantaleon; Amalfi, the body of Saint Andrew. An English priest brought a relic of the True Cross back to Bromholm, in Norfolk, where it was venerated as "the Rood of

Under the aegis of the Byzantine emperors, art and theology fused to create some of the world's most opulent religious objects. Below is the sixth-century ivory throne of Maximian, the Archbishop of Ravenna. Every inch is carved with birds, animals, scenes from the life of Christ, and the story of Joseph in Egypt; the panels below the seat depict Saint John the Baptist and the four Evangelists. In the tenth century, Emperor Constantine VII Porphyrogenitus commissioned an enameled receptacle (overleaf) for a relic of the True Cross. Both the outer (left) and inner (right) containers are of silver gilt, set with jeweled and cloisonné ornaments.

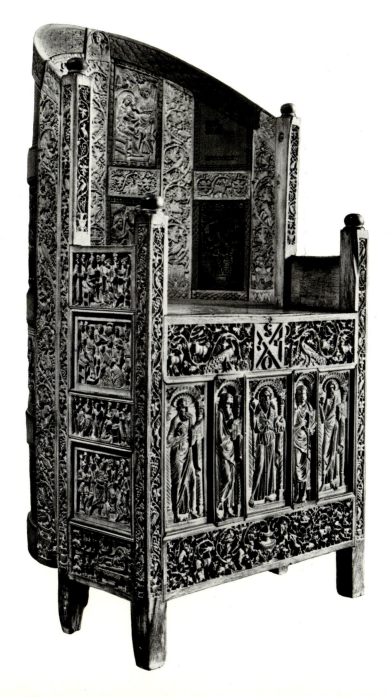

Bromholm" (to which reference is made in *Piers Plowman*).

A finely wrought Byzantine reliquary, made for Constantine Porphyrogenitus to contain another piece of the True Cross, found its way to the German city of Limburg an der Lahn, where it reposes today. Some years later the Crown of Thorns was pawned to the Venetians and came into the hands of Louis IX — Saint Louis, as the French monarch was known after his canonization in 1297. Louis built the Sainte-Chapelle in Paris to enshrine the Crown of Thorns along with such other relics as a portion of the True Cross, baby linen worn by Christ, the chain of his Passion, the lance, the sponge, the rod of Moses, and yet another part of the skull of Saint John the Baptist — relics sold by a subsequent Latin emperor who ran short of funds.

Under the terms of the covenant, the major share of the reliquaries fell to Venice. Many still reside in the treasury of Saint Mark's, including yet another portion of the Baptist's skull. Among its thirty-two Byzantine chalices made from such semiprecious stones as agate, onyx, sardonyx, chalcedony, and rock crystal, are many from Hagia Sophia and other churches in Constantinople. A Venetian historian writes of "the many holy relics, and small figures, and chalices and patens and other beautiful things" that came from Hagia Sophia, as did "the very same doors which now close the church of Saint Mark's." The great gold-paneled altarpiece of Saint Mark's, the *Pala d'Oro,* made in Constantinople in the tenth century and enlarged in the twelfth, was completed in the thirteenth by the addition of enamels and precious stones from Hagia Sophia and elsewhere. One of its panels — perhaps coincidentally — embodies

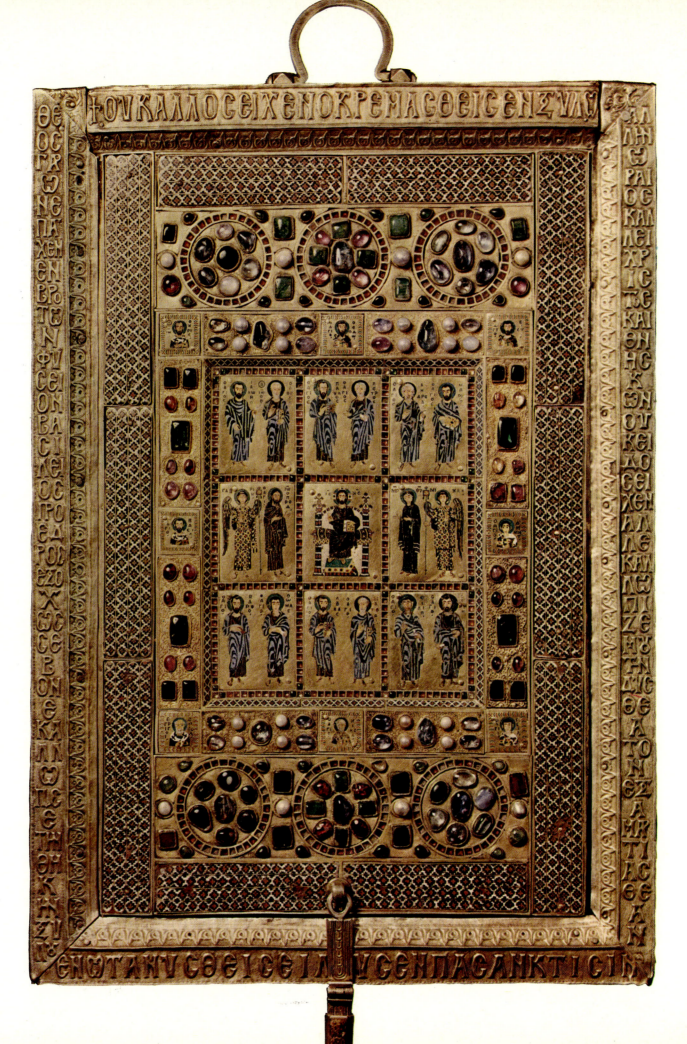

a figure of Solomon with the Greek inscription, "Wisdom hath builded her house."

Outstanding among the classical masterpieces acquired by Venice were the four bronze horses, cast in imperial Rome and later sent to Constantinople, that may once have graced the Hippodrome and now crown the central entrance of Saint Mark's. The porphyry columns on which they stand may likewise have come at this time from Constantinople. In any event, Saint Mark's presently incorporates, both on its outer façades and interior surfaces, numerous columns, capitals, carvings, and panels of marble looted from Constantinople in 1204. Even before the fall of the city, the south façade of Saint Mark's, which overlooks the water, was traditionally devoted to displays of the spoils from the republic's various wars — placed so as to impress the visitor arriving from abroad. From 1204 on, the architectural development of Saint Mark's was essentially Byzantine in style.

After the sack of Constantinople, the Doge of Venice was honored with a resounding Latin title meaning "Ruler of a quarter and half a quarter of the Roman Empire." And indeed, for the next half century Venice was the real power behind the Latin "Empire of Romania." After the Venetians had received their territorial share — which amounted to three-eighths of the Byzantine lands, three-eighths of the city of Constantinople itself, and most of the best harbors — only a quarter was left for the emperor. The remaining three-eighths of the Latin share was distributed among his knights in the form of fiefs.

By the choice of the Crusaders and with the approval of the Venetians, Baldwin, Count of Flanders and Hainaut, became the first Latin emperor and was crowned in Hagia Sophia on May 16, 1204, three weeks after Easter. "And you must know," records Villehardouin, "that many a rich robe was made for the coronation; nor did they want for the wherewithal." Borne aloft on a shield — a pre-Christian tradition — Baldwin proceeded to the church, where he was invested with the scarlet imperial buskins. Later he was crowned by the papal legate, who employed the rites of both the Latin and Orthodox churches. The quarter of the city that included Hagia Sophia formed part of the Venetian domain. Thus a Venetian patriarch, Thomas Morosini, was soon installed in the church with Venetian clergy. When the doge died shortly thereafter he was buried in Hagia Sophia, where a stone still commemorates him.

Already restricted territorially, the Latin emperor's power was further limited politically — by a constitution based on a combination of feudal theory and the supposed practice of the kingdom of Jerusalem. Under this system, Baldwin became little more than the chairman of a council of tenants-in-chief who advised him on policy, directed military operations, and had the power of veto over his administrative decisions, while a high court regulated his relations with his vassals.

After the conquest, many of the Greek churches in Constantinople were converted to the Latin rite, but few were destroyed. Indeed, Hagia Sophia underwent, at the hands of the Latins, a much-needed restoration. Throughout its lifetime the great church had endured numerous earthquake shocks following the first one, which had brought down the dome in Justinian's time.

The Doge of Venice pledged both men and funds for the Fourth Crusade from the pulpit of Saint Mark's — the cathedral that was to become the major repository of booty from Constantinople. Among the city's treasures that found their way to Saint Mark's are the four bronze horses (left) that now stand on the parapet of the façade.

Twenty-three quakes were recorded between the beginning of the seventh and the middle of the fifteenth century, and each of these had left its mark. In the latter part of the ninth century, a restoration was undertaken by Basil I when the broad, lofty western arch began to show rents and threatened to collapse. Basil's workmen girded the arch with iron bands and rebuilt it. Nevertheless, in 989, at a time when the church was not in use, a shock of exceptional severity brought down this western arch and the semidome. Its rebuilding under Basil II took eight years to complete.

During the eleventh century there were ten earthquake shocks of varying severity. Although the twelfth century had been free from shocks, the Crusaders found the structure of the church to be in a precarious condition at the outset of the thirteenth century. As practical Westerners, skilled in the art of building — and especially in the new science of thrust and counterthrust in relation to high arches and vaults — they undoubtedly took steps to secure its stability. Latin chroniclers of the time found other matters more worthy of record, and the Greeks would hardly give credit for such work to the conqueror. Ironic as the notion may seem, the Latin rulers of Constantinople may well have been responsible for Hagia Sophia's ultimate survival.

Their chief contribution consisted, it seems, of much-needed buttresses to support the western end of the building. Of the original eight or ten flying buttresses along this façade, some have been altered, reinforced, or reconstructed in subsequent times. One seems to have remained unaltered, however, and that resembles the Gothic buttresses of the thirteenth-century structures in the Île-de-France so closely as to prompt the conclusion that it was built during the Latin occupation. If this is so, the neighboring buttresses may also date from the Latin period, forming part of a skillful scientific scheme for the external stabilization of a vaulting system weakened by earthquake shocks and subsequent neglect.

It was also, with reasonable certainty, the Latins who, finding no church bells in Hagia Sophia, erected a belfry supported by buttress-piers in the center of the west façade. That high rectangular tower has vanished, but according to eyewitness accounts it was standing in the seventeenth century after the Turks had melted down its bells to make cannon.

The Latin empire lasted for barely two generations. An alien, feudal growth that failed to root itself in the imperial Greek soil, it carried within itself the seeds of its own disintegration. Of its four emperors only one, Henry of Flanders, contrived to rise above the level of a mere premier baron among disparate peers forever in rivalry over the fiefs and petty kingdoms that proliferated as time went on. The short-lived regime was never an imperial power as the Byzantine Empire had been and was to become once again. Nor did it ever extend far beyond the confines of Europe — where the most manageable and profitable bases were in any case held by the Serene Republic of Venice.

The Greeks on the other hand, with their contrasting energy of spirit, practical talent, and resilience in the face of disaster, were quick to revive their independent authority in Asia. Within two years of the fall

In an elaborate ceremony at Hagia Sophia that
included both Latin and Orthodox rites, Baldwin
of Flanders (right) was crowned first emperor of
"Romania." His control over the truncated empire
and its recalcitrant Greek subjects was precarious
at best, however, and within sixty years the
Byzantines managed to reconquer Constantinople.

of Constantinople they had regained most of their
western Asian lands. They had even established suc-
cessor-states: one, under the Comnenes, at Trebizond
on the shores of the Black Sea; another at Nicaea,
under Anna Comnena, the daughter of Alexius III,
and her husband, Theodore Lascaris, who had prudently rejected the last-minute offer of the imperial
throne to cross into Asia as the capital fell. At Nicaea,
Anna and Theodore were joined by a large group of
leading citizens who had likewise escaped from the
city, and the clergy among them elected a new patriarch
who crowned them emperor and empress. In Europe
a Greek despotate was established in Epirus under a
bastard of the Angeli. This state was to serve as the
bridgehead for the recapture of Thessalonica and
other parts of the Balkan peninsula at the expense of
the Latins. Epirus was curbed in due course by Nicaea,
which had achieved a constructive alliance with
Bulgaria. Thus, by the middle of the thirteenth century
the Latin capital of Constantinople had been effectively
isolated and virtually encircled by the vigorous Greek
regime of Nicaea.

The last Latin emperor, Baldwin II, was reduced to
a state of poverty, and sought help from all sides. He
not only pawned the Crown of Thorns and other
relics to the Venetians, but on one occasion he even
placed his own son Philip in Venetian hands as a pledge
for a loan. In a series of "mendicant visits" to the
Western courts, he sought men or money for the relief
of his sinking empire. Politely if coldly received, he
met with little or no success. "But how often," writes
Gibbon, "was the exile, the vagrant, the imperial
beggar humbled with scorn, insulted with pity, and

degraded in his own eyes and those of the nations!"
Meanwhile, in Constantinople the standard of living
declined, poverty and famine became rife, lead was
stripped from the palace roofs to cover day-to-day
expenses, and buildings were demolished to obtain
timber for fuel. The city degenerated into a "dreary
prospect of solitude and ruin":

> The palace was defiled with smoke and dirt, and the
> gross intemperance of the Franks; whole streets had
> been consumed by fire, or were decayed by the injuries
> of time; the sacred and profane edifices were stripped
> of their ornaments; and, as if they were conscious of
> their approaching exile, the industry of the Latins
> had been confined to the work of pillage and destruc-
> tion. Trade had expired under the pressure of anarchy
> and distress; and the number of inhabitants had de-
> creased with the opulence of the city.

Such was the condition of Constantinople when the
Greeks recaptured the city — almost by accident — in
the summer of 1261. The Venetian fleet had temporarily left the Golden Horn to carry out an operation on
the Black Sea coast, and a Byzantine general on recon-
naissance in Thrace was surprised to find the land walls
virtually undefended. A loyal Greek drugged the sen-
tries at the Silivri Gate; a force of a mere eight hundred
soldiers climbed up over the fortifications, surprised
and killed the half-asleep Latin guards, broke down the
barricades, and opened the gate from within; and the
Greek army marched into the city. The Latin emperor,
the patriarch, and the Venetian settlers fled. And thus,
by an extraordinarily fortunate and all but bloodless
coup de main, the city of Constantinople was restored
to the Byzantine Empire.

V

The Fall of Constantinople

News of the unexpected capitulation of Constantinople was brought to Emperor Michael Palaeologus in his palace near Smyrna by a messenger carrying — as proof of his claim — the sword and scepter, the scarlet buskins, and the bonnet dropped by Baldwin II in his precipitate flight. Before an assembly of bishops, senators, and nobles, the emperor declared: "The Divine Providence has now restored to our arms the city of Constantine, the sacred seat of religion and empire; and it will depend on our valor and conduct to render this important acquisition the pledge and omen of future victories."

Twenty days later Michael Palaeologus, who had already been crowned emperor in Nicaea, made his triumphal entry into the half-ruined city through the Golden Gate. Surrounded by his people and preceded by an image of the Virgin, he went on foot to the monastery of Saint John of Stoudion, where he gave thanks to the Almighty. He was then crowned for a second time, as Michael VIII, in Hagia Sophia. So began the reign of the Palaeologi, the last dynasty of the Byzantine Empire, which was to endure for two additional centuries.

The revived empire was only a shadow of its former self, but in the fourteenth century it was suffused with the twilight glow of a cultural renaissance comparable to that which was dawning in Italy. Territorially reduced by the inexorable westward advance of the Turks in Asia Minor, politically divided by dynastic and theological disputes, economically impoverished, socially disturbed, and decimated by the Black Death, which had reduced its population by a third, the latter-day empire nonetheless flourished anew in terms of intellectual and artistic accomplishment. Scholars and artists abounded; philosophers, scientists, doctors, mathematicians, astronomers, theologians, and historians brought new life to the Hellenic tradition. Simultaneously, artist-craftsmen, sculptors, painters, jewelers, and mosaicists raised their art to new heights. New churches were built, smaller in scale but often richer aesthetically than the old. State patronage of the arts — virtually nonexistent under an impoverished court that had been reduced to periodically selling its jewels and treasures, and to eating off earthenware and pewter instead of gold and silver plate — began to give way to the private patronage of rich citizens who commissioned mosaics, frescoes, icons, and even the decoration of entire churches.

Even during those lean years, Hagia Sophia remained the imperial church, which made the state responsible for its upkeep. Soon after his recapture of the city, Michael VIII refounded the university in Hagia Sophia's outbuildings. In the church itself, he restored much of the damage done by the Crusaders: the elaborate doors of the three royal gates, which had been removed, were replaced by bronze doors of a simpler design; the bema, ambo, and solea were restored at the emperor's expense; and the church was enriched with vestments and sacred vessels. This involved the replacement of "furnishings of surpassing beauty" that the Crusaders had removed and the restoration of the iconostasis, from which they had stripped the silver plating.

Michael VIII's son and successor, Andronicus II, carried out important works to stabilize the external structure of the church. In 1317, when he learned from

his engineers that the northern and eastern walls were dangerously weakened and would give way unless strengthened, he built pyramidal tower-buttresses to support the vaults at points of stress. These rose to the full height of the building. Unnecessarily bulky in scale — and, moreover, clumsy in design — they sadly deface the aspect and distort the proportions of the exterior of Hagia Sophia today.

In 1344, a major earthquake caused ominous subsidence and opened new cracks in the structure. This led, two years later, to the collapse of the eastern arch together with the eastern part of the dome. "It was now evening," records the fourteenth-century Byzantine historian Nicephorus Gregoras, "and not far from midnight, with the sky calm and clear, when one of the four lofty arches — that which looks toward the rising sun — fell to the ground, dragging with it the adjacent vaults." Another historian adds: "When the whole city had rushed to the site of the catastrophe and had wept for the misfortune, they began straight away to carry forth the ruined material, working unremittingly, both men and women, for thirty days and nights."

The church's restoration, the last of any importance to be undertaken by the Greeks, took ten years to complete because of the civil strife and economic confusion that then gripped the Byzantine Empire. The Greeks, as their efforts indicate, had come to appreciate Western building skills. They completed the buttressing operation begun by the Latins a century earlier and achieved a degree of permanent stabilization for the structure of Hagia Sophia.

When the eastern wall fell, the bema was destroyed and the iconostasis itself collapsed — obliterating much of the restoration work done by Michael VIII. The sacred icons were restored by the Empress Anna, widow of Andronicus III, who is accused by a contemporary historian of having previously robbed the church of furniture and ornaments.

According to Ruy González de Clavijo, the Spanish ambassador to the Byzantine court, the new ambo — the fourth and last to be built — rested "on four columns of jasper and had its walls sheathed with many slabs of jasper and marbles of varied hue; and this pulpit was entirely covered by a dome carried on eight large columns of parti-coloured jasper." The mosaics were restored later by the Emperor John Palaeologus who, in commemoration of his work, was himself portrayed in mosaic in the eastern arch. The Virgin and Child in the apse required such extensive restoration that they must for all intents and purposes be dated from the fourteenth century. As such, they are among the last major works of Byzantine art to be created in Hagia Sophia before the Turkish conquest.

Meanwhile, other sacred relics had been acquired for Hagia Sophia to replace those lost to the Franks. A Russian pilgrim of the fifteenth century found such treasures in plenty, and he enumerates them in detail, as his predecessors of earlier centuries had done. They included an image of the Virgin that had purportedly wept when the Franks occupied the city; a coffer of pearls, representing her tears, stood before it. A French traveler named de Broquière, visiting Hagia Sophia in 1433, identified "one of the robes of our Lord, the end of the lance that pierced his side, the sponge that was offered to him, and the reed that was put in his hand" among the instruments of the Passion

In a desperate attempt to win assistance from the Christian West in his struggle against the Turks — whose growing militancy threatened the continued existence of his empire — John VIII Palaeologus, accompanied by the Patriarch of Constantinople, journeyed to Florence in 1439. During the ensuing negotiations over a proposed act of union with Rome, leading Italian artists were captivated by the exotic attire of the Eastern emperor and his entourage. Antonio Pisanello made a striking portrait medallion (left), in which the emperor's proud profile is accentuated by his wide-brimmed hat. Benozzo Gozzoli portrayed John VIII in a fresco of The Procession of the Magi (detail below) for a palace in Florence. The detail at right, from Filarete's bronze doors at Saint Peter's in Rome, depicts the emperor embarking for the return trip to Constantinople.

that were regularly displayed inside the great church.

As the empire entered its final decline, Hagia Sophia became progressively more neglected. A few years after the coronation of Manuel II Palaeologus – third from the end of the imperial line – in 1391, the Spanish ambassador González de Clavijo wrote that "the outer gates by which the church was approached are broken and fallen." In the last years of the emperor's reign, the Florentine traveler Buondelmonti got the impression that "only the dome of the Church remained, as everything is fallen down and in ruins." By the fifteenth century Constantinople was a sadly diminished city. One foreign traveler was astonished to find it so full of ruins, another was aghast at its emptiness, and a third remarked on its sparse and impoverished population. The great bazaars were almost devoid of produce, the great warehouses derelict and infested with rats. Many quarters of the city, once built-up and prosperous, had reverted to nature, with birds singing and wild flowers blooming in orchards and hedgerows. Such were the last stages of a decline that had its roots in the Latin conquest.

The Turks took full and vigorous advantage of Constantinople's plight. The Seljuks had given way to a new tribal dynasty – the Ottoman – that had first crossed into Europe in 1345. Within two decades they had established a European capital at Adrianople, and by 1373 the Byzantine emperor was paying a vassal's tribute to the Ottoman sultan. By the turn of the fifteenth century, the Turks were preparing to march on Constantinople. Providentially, they were interrupted when Tamerlane the Tatar invaded their Asian dominions from the east. Thus the encircled and in-creasingly desperate city was granted a fifty-year respite.

A brief siege of Constantinople was raised in 1422 because of internal dissension among the Ottomans, giving Eastern and Western Christendom a last chance to form a coalition against the infidel. Lamentably, the rulers of the West were too disunited politically and the people of the East too united theologically – and too reluctant to forgive the Latins and so heal the schism that divided their respective churches – for this to succeed. Two attempts at a revived Crusade ended in military failure. A succession of Byzantine emperors, acutely aware that only Western help could save their empire, sought a compromise in terms of union between the two churches, but it was soon evident that such a union could only be achieved through the submission of the Greek Church to Rome and to the demands of the papacy – and this the people of the Byzantine Empire would never accept.

In 1439, on the initiative of Emperor John VIII and at the invitation of Pope Eugene IV, an ecumenical council was held at Florence to discuss the question of union with Rome. An Act of Union was eventually agreed upon between the papal legates and the Greek delegation of bishops – but it was greeted with bitter hostility in Constantinople, where it was rejected as being, in effect, a statement of Latin doctrine, allowing only for certain Greek usages. "The clergy," wrote Gibbon, "confident in their orthodoxy and science, had promised themselves and their flocks an easy victory over the blind shepherds. . . . What had been the event or use of their Italian synod? They answered, with sighs and tears, 'Alas! We have made a new faith; we have exchanged piety for impiety; we have betrayed

Although the Latin invaders were driven from Constantinople in 1261, the Byzantine Empire never fully recovered from that defeat. By the middle of the fifteenth century, the impoverished and highly vulnerable city was ripe for conquest — and in 1453 it fell easy prey to the well-trained armies of Sultan Mohammed II. Gentile Bellini's portrait (right) captures the forceful and dynamic personality of the young Ottoman ruler.

the immaculate sacrifice.'" Soon afterward, the last of the Byzantine emperors, Constantine XI Palaeologus, came to the throne.

By 1452 the imminence of another Turkish siege was apparent to all. At the end of that year, in a final, desperate bid for Western support, the Act of Union was proclaimed in Hagia Sophia in the presence of the emperor and the papal legate but in the absence of the patriarch. The leading opponent of union was Gennadius II, a revered Orthodox churchman and scholar who had withdrawn to a monastery. When members of the opposition came to consult him in his cell, he handed them a note asking why they put their trust in the Italians rather than God. It declared that in losing their faith they would surely lose their city and predicted a future of enslavement to the Azymites — those who celebrated with unleavened bread. While rioters swept through the streets of Constantinople, a mass was sung in Hagia Sophia. Roman and Greek priests took part, the cardinal preached a sermon, and the congregation formally, if conditionally, accepted the union.

From that moment, few Greek worshipers set foot in Hagia Sophia, where only the priests who accepted the union were permitted to serve. The Grand Duke Lucas Notaras, Senior Minister of the Crown, went so far as to declare that a sultan's turban was preferable to a cardinal's hat, and the historian Michael Ducas spoke of the church as no better than a Jewish synagogue or heathen temple. With passive reluctance, the bulk of the populace accepted the union as an accomplished fact but continued to worship only in churches whose priests had not agreed to it. Nor did the Act of Union

lead to the appearance of Western military aid. For the sake of their material safety, the Greeks compromised with their spiritual conscience over a creed that they believed to be divinely ordained. They had paid the price — only to see themselves cheated. In a spirit of fatalism they awaited the fall of an empire whose days had long since been numbered by divinely inspired prophecy.

In 1451 a shrewd and ambitious young sultan, Mohammed II, had succeeded to the Ottoman throne. From his boyhood he had dreamed of conquering Constantinople, an objective that his predecessors had failed to achieve. His intention was made abundantly clear by the swift construction of the castle of Rumeli Hisar on the European shore of the Bosporus as a base for his operations. Known to fifteenth-century Turks as Boghaz-Kesen — cutter of the strait or of the throat — the new fortress stood to the north of the city at the narrowest point of the channel, opposite the earlier fortress of Anadolu Hisar, which guarded the Asian shore. When the castle was completed at the end of August 1452, the sultan marched his troops out through its gates and up to the walls of Constantinople to reconnoiter the Greek fortifications. At the same time he ordered that all ships passing through the Bosporus must stop at Rumeli Hisar for inspection; otherwise they would be fired upon and sunk.

The sultan then returned to his capital at Adrianople, where he embarked on clandestine preparations for his projected siege. Unable to sleep, Mohammed is said to have tramped the streets at night disguised as an ordinary soldier, sounding out the opinions of his men and killing any who ventured to recognize and

salute him. One night, when his vizier appeared bearing a customary gift of gold coins, Mohammed swept them aside, exclaiming, "Only one thing I want. Give me Constantinople." Revealing this objective to his council of ministers, the sultan declared that if he could not rule an empire that contained Constantinople, he would prefer not to rule an empire at all.

Previous sieges of the city had been made from the landward side only, he emphasized, and had failed because the Greeks could receive supplies by sea. But the Turks were no longer dependent on the fleets of the Christian powers. They had a navy of their own, a Turkish armada composed of some 125 ships — five times as many as the Greeks could muster in the Golden Horn by pooling their own resources with those of the Venetians, the Genoese, and other European peoples.

The army that Mohammed assembled in Thrace consisted of some 100,000 men, of whom 20,000 were irregulars. The spearhead of his troops was a force of 12,000 Janissaries, a disciplined elite trained to act either as infantry or cavalry. Recruited not from among the Turks but from selected Christian subjects who were removed from their families in boyhood to be brought up as devout Moslems, these fearsome warriors served only the sultan.

Besides such familiar medieval weapons as the bow and arrow, harquebus, catapult, lance, and scimitar, the Turkish army was equipped — by a sultan assiduous in his study of scientific progress — with up-to-date artillery fired by gunpowder. Although this explosive had been used in Western Europe for over a century, it was still unfamiliar in the Middle East. It thus pro-

vided the shrewd sultan with an advantage over the Greeks that was as much psychological as tactical. His prize piece of artillery was a cannon powerful enough, in the words of its maker, a Hungarian engineer named Urban, to blast the walls of Babylon itself. Ironically enough, Urban had first offered his services to the emperor, but Mohammed had secured them by quadrupling his expected salary and providing him with all the raw material and technical assistance he needed.

This monster weapon, whose fame soon spread far and wide, had a barrel more than twenty-six feet long and eight inches in diameter, and its stone cannonballs were said to weigh more than 1,300 pounds. When the roads to Constantinople had been leveled and the bridges strengthened, the great cannon was brought from Adrianople. Rumbling through Thrace on a gun-carriage drawn by sixty oxen and accompanied by two hundred men, the cannon finally arrived at a point five miles from the walls of Constantinople. Other, smaller cannon, cast in the sultan's own foundries, were also rolled into place. Against such an up-to-date armory, the stone walls of Constantinople, erected in the Middle Ages, no longer provided an adequate means of defense.

Such was the force that a Greek army of no more than seven thousand men, two thousand of whom were foreigners, was to confront across fourteen miles of walls on April 5, 1453. The Greeks were equipped only with light cannon — largely for fear of damaging their own walls — and they were short both of powder and of arms. The Venetian colony, established in the city for centuries, hastened to contribute troops and ships for its defense and that of "the honor of God and

The formidable Turkish army — whose banners were emblazoned with the Moslem crescent — was spearheaded by an elite corps of former Christians, raised from birth as fanatical fighting men and known as Janissaries. At left is a sketch by Gentile Bellini of one such professional soldier.

Christendom." However, six of their ships slipped ignominiously away before the siege, carrying with them seven hundred men.

The Genoese, although their interests were in conflict with those of the Venetians, prepared to fight for the Christian cause nonetheless. They were reinforced by the timely arrival of a prominent Genoese soldier and nobleman, Giovanni Giustiniani, and his band of seven hundred well-armed men. Renowned for his skill in the defense of walled cities, Giustiniani was engaged by the emperor to be the city's commander in chief. He was promised the island of Lemnos as a reward in the event of victory. The new commander in chief set to work at once, surveying the defenses and strengthening the walls, while all the arms in the city were collected for redistribution. With the emperor's personal encouragement, Christians of both sexes labored throughout the winter to clear the moats and repair the walls, patching them with tombstones and any other materials on which they could lay their hands.

With the approach of spring, Mohammed began to march his great army through Thrace to the Bosporus. Supremely confident, the sultan and his last detachment arrived before the walls of the city. The morale of his troops was fortified by hopes of a special place in paradise, one foreshadowed by Moslem tradition: "They shall conquer Qostantiniya [Constantinople]. Glory be to the prince and to the army that shall achieve it." The Prophet himself had inquired of his disciples: "Have you heard of a city of which one side is land and the two others sea? The hour of Judgment shall not sound until 70,000 sons of Isaac [followers of Mohammed] shall capture it."

Throughout a hard winter the Greeks — visited ominously by earthquakes, torrential rains, floods, lightning, and shooting stars — had remembered, with a fatalism which nonetheless bred courage, prophecies of the end of the empire and the coming of the anti-Christ. When diplomatic exchanges with the sultan came to naught, the emperor wrote to him:

As it is clear that you desire war more than peace, since I cannot satisfy you either by my protestations of sincerity, or by my readiness to swear allegiance, so let it be according to your desire. I turn now and look to God alone. Should it be His will that the city be yours, where is he who can oppose it? If He should inspire you with a desire for Peace, I shall be only too happy. However, I release you from all your oaths and treaties with me, and, closing the gates of my capital, I will defend my people to the last drop of my blood. Reign in happiness until the All-Just, the Supreme God, calls us both before His judgment seat.

The gates of the city were sealed. A boom in the form of a chain on wooden floats was stretched across the entrance to the harbor of the Golden Horn by the Genoese. The people of the city prayed in Hagia Sophia and other churches throughout Holy Week. As it came to a close the sultan, conforming to Islamic law, sent messengers under a flag of truce to make a final offer of peace to the citizens. In return for their voluntary surrender, he offered them freedom of life and property under his protection. They refused to surrender, and on April 6 the bombardment began. A week later it was intensified, and it continued unabated for six additional weeks.

For all their superiority in arms and manpower, the

The oldest surviving map of Constantinople and its environs (below left), executed slightly more than three decades before the Turkish siege of 1453, reveals the extraordinary combination of natural defenses and man-made battlements that rendered the Byzantine capital practically invulnerable for a full millennium. Girdled on three sides by water, the city presented only one flank to Mohammed's ground troops — and that western border was buttressed by a double line of stout fortifications. From Hagia Sophia (center), the city's defenders were to watch in horror as the sultan's troops dragged warships across the Pera peninsula (top) and into the Golden Horn. Exposed to attack on two sides, Constantinople finally capitulated to Mohammed's Janissary guard, pictured at lower right in conical white turbans.

attacking forces did not at first make notable progress. On the landward side, the Turkish artillery failed to effect any decisive breach, although its huge cannonballs destroyed the walls at many points and demolished a number of towers. The Greeks, under Giustiniani, were quick to repair the damage and to strengthen the weakened portions, even resorting to the use of bales of wool and sheets of leather for this purpose. More effective was the erection, at a point where the Ottoman threat was greatest, of a jerry-built stockade constructed out of stout wooden planks and barrels filled with tamped soil.

At sea, the Turkish fleet twice failed to force the boom protecting the Golden Horn. Moreover, a Genoese supply fleet, after an all-day naval battle in full view of the city's inhabitants, succeeded by superior seamanship in defeating the Turks and safely entering the shelter of the Golden Horn. Humiliated by this setback, the sultan boldly transported a fleet of some seventy ships overland. Using wheeled cradles and an improvised "tramway" of timber, his men dragged the Ottoman fleet across the Pera peninsula from the Bosporus into the Golden Horn. This resourceful operation, probably suggested to the sultan by an Italian in his service, neatly outflanked both the boom and the Greek fleet. A counterattack by the Venetians and Genoese failed, and the Greeks lost control of the Golden Horn — a vital blow that strengthened Turkish communications, hampered Genoese support, and fatally weakened the defense of both the harbor and the city's land walls.

By the beginning of May provisions in the city began to run short and the strain on the defenders became

Virtually impregnable land walls (right), built by Theodosius II in the fifth century, had protected Constantinople from attack for a thousand years. In 1453 the fortifications were finally breached by the inexorable Ottoman advance, and today they stand in crumbling isolation.

evident. Friction grew between the Venetians and the Genoese, their traditional rivals. The emperor was advised by some to leave the city and organize resistance from outside. After listening quietly and patiently, he spoke to his subjects:

> I thank you all for the advice which you have given me. . . . But it is impossible for me to go away: how could I leave the churches of our Lord, and His servants the clergy, and the throne, and my people in such a plight? What would the world say of me? I pray you, my friends, in future do not say to me anything else but Nay, Sire, do not leave us. Never, never will I leave you. I am resolved to die here with you.

His eyes filled with tears, Constantine avowed his intention "to follow the example of the Good Shepherd who lays down his life for his sheep."

Some weeks earlier a swift Venetian brigantine, its crew disguised as Turks, had been sent out to seek the fleet of reinforcements that had been promised from Venice. It returned without finding a trace of the fleet. No help for Eastern Christendom — not a man, not a penny — was to come from the Christian West. The city, Emperor Constantine said, could only put its faith in Christ, His mother, and Saint Constantine.

But no help was to come from Heaven either, it seemed. Prophecies had foretold that the last Christian emperor would be named Constantine, as the first had been, and a series of natural and supernatural portents seemed to confirm them. There was an eclipse of the full moon, and Constantinople was plunged into three hours of unnatural darkness; a holy icon of the protecting Virgin, which slipped off its platform while being carried in procession, proved almost impossible

to lift, having suddenly become as heavy as lead. A thunderstorm flooded the streets, and then a thick fog engulfed the city. Was the Divinity shrouding himself to conceal his departure? When the fog lifted, a great light, like a sign from the heavens, was seen to envelop the dome of Hagia Sophia. Here was an omen that alarmed even the sultan — until his wise men identified it as the light of the True Faith, which would soon shine through the sacred building.

Nonetheless, there was hesitation among the Turks. They made several attempts to mine the walls and bridge the moat, but without effect, and after nearly seven weeks of siege no Turkish soldier had yet set foot inside the city. Among the troops there was a spirit of frustration and a drop in morale. The sultan's older advisers were prudently pacific; his younger officers were urgently belligerent. Mohammed made a last bid for peace with the emperor, offering him a choice between the payment of a heavy annual tribute and the forced evacuation of the citizens of Constantinople to a kingdom in Peloponnesus. The emperor refused both. The sultan retorted that the only choices remaining to the Greeks were the surrender of their city, conversion to Islam, or death by the sword.

On May 25, 1453, the sultan gave orders for a final all-out assault on the walls. Heralds proclaimed it as Mohammed paraded between the ranks of his soldiery, promising them three days of license to sack the captured city. From within the walls, the Greeks could hear their jubilant cry: "There is no God but Allah, and Mohammed is his Prophet!" On the eve of the assault, the young sultan addressed a brief exhortation to his pashas:

The news of Constantinople's capitulation
prompted one French miniaturist to produce his
own somewhat fanciful version of the siege.
Through the artist's active but insular imagination,
the city became a fortified European town — and
Hagia Sophia (center) a Gothic cathedral. Despite
these discrepancies, this contemporary view does
reveal a number of key aspects of Mohammed's
battle plan: the route by which the sultan's warships
were transported across Pera (left), the barrel bridge
that linked the Turkish encampment (bottom) to
the mainland, and the awesome array of artillery
that eventually ruptured the renowned land walls.

I give you today a grand and populous city, the capital of the ancient Romans, the very summit of splendour and of glory, which has become, so to say, the centre of the world. I give it over for you to pillage, to seize its incalculable treasures of men, women, and boys, and everything that adorns it. You will henceforward live in great happiness and leave great wealth to your children.

By the light of flares and torches — and to the sound of trumpets, fifes, and drums — the Turks labored to fill in the moat and pile up arms before the walls. Throughout the following day a total and ominous silence reigned outside the walls. Within them, it was broken by the pealing of church bells and the sounding of gongs — as icons and relics were carried in procession through the streets and around the inner perimeter, with pauses for prayer at the points where the damage was greatest. In this calm before the storm, the citizens of Constantinople forgot their disputes. Greeks, Venetians, and Genoese paraded together, and Orthodox and Catholic alike sang hymns and joined in the Kyrie Eleison.

The emperor himself took part in the procession. Afterward he delivered to the chief citizens, Greek and Italian, what Gibbon describes as "the funeral oration of the Roman Empire." Constantine's companion and chronicler, Phrantzes, quotes the embattled emperor as saying: "Brothers and fellow-citizens, be ready for the morn. If God gives us grace and valour, and the Holy Trinity help us, in whom alone we trust, we will do such deeds that the foe shall fall back in shame before our arms." He turned to the Venetians and Genoese, whom he hailed as "our companions, our faithful allies, and our brethren." Then, we are told, "the wretched Romans strengthened their hearts like lions, sought and gave pardon, and with tears embraced each other as though mindful no more of wife or children or worldly goods, but only of death, which they were glad to undergo."

The crowds moved toward the great church of Hagia Sophia, "to strengthen themselves by prayer and the reception of the Holy Mysteries, to confirm their vows to fight, and, if need be, mindless of all worldly interests, to die for the honor of God and Christianity." In the five months since the Act of Union was established, no pious Greek had entered the church, which was thought to be defiled by the Latin rite. But that night all gathered to partake in the liturgy, regardless of the schism. As the vespers service was sung in Hagia Sophia for the last time, patriarch and cardinal, Greek and Latin clergy, and a full congregation of citizens united beneath the glittering mosaics and the myriads of candles and lamps to confess and communicate together in a last intercession for their city's salvation.

Later that same night the emperor, having bid farewell to his ministers and commanders, rode back to the great church. After praying with fervor, he prostrated himself before the figures of Christ and the Madonna in the iconostasis and made his own peace with God. Constantine then returned to his palace to rest, begging all those present to pardon him. "What a weeping there was then and what a bewailing in the palace!" wrote Phrantzes. "Had one been made of wood or of stone, one would still have had to weep with them." After a final tour of the walls, he took up his post by the Gate of Saint Romanus to the muffled

sound of the Turks preparing scaling ladders in the moat outside.

At 1:30 A.M. on May 29, the Turkish assault was launched with a sudden pandemonium of sound: shrill battle cries echoed above the booming of cannon, the clashing of cymbals, the blasting of trumpets, and the wailing of fifes. Instantly this din was augmented by the clang of church bells, as the men on the walls gave the alarm and it was spread throughout the city. Within minutes the crowds still worshiping in Hagia Sophia realized that the battle had started. Fighting men ran to their posts, women hurried after them to carry the stones and beams needed to strengthen the walls, and others remained in the great church to pray for deliverance.

At the walls there was no time for prayer. The attack came in three successive waves: first the irregulars, who were checked and repulsed after two hours; then the more disciplined regimental troops — too numerous for so narrow a front — who suffered heavy losses as the Greeks hurled back their scaling ladders, flung stones down upon them, and fought them hand-to-hand. After four hours of slaughter the Turkish troops began to grow weary and the Janissaries were ordered forward. Advancing in unbroken ranks to the ring of martial music, the sultan's elite warriors tore and hacked at the stockade, which had been broken at several points by balls from the great cannon.

The progress made by the Janissaries was nevertheless slow, and the Greeks fought tenaciously until two fatal misfortunes befell them. First, a detachment of Turkish troops found that a small postern gate in a corner of the walls had been left open by the defenders after a sortie against the enemy's flanks. Before it could be closed a number of Turks ran through it and started to climb the tower above. At the same time Giustiniani, commanding the defense of the walls, received a severe and painful wound. Despite Constantine's pleas, he insisted upon leaving the battle, and his men carried him through the city streets and down to a ship that lay at anchor in the harbor.

Giustiniani's departure caused a demoralization amounting to panic among the Christian troops, who shouted, "The Turks have got in!" Taking advantage of their fear, the sultan cried, "We have the city; it is ours; the wall is undefended!" Thus encouraged, the Janissaries charged once more — and this time reached the top of the damaged stockade. At that moment the Turkish flag was seen flying from the tower above the postern gate, and the Greek cry went up, "The city is taken." Soon tens of thousands of ravening Turkish troops were swarming across Constantinople's battered walls and into the streets of the city itself.

Mounting his Arabian mare, the emperor galloped toward the postern gate, but it was too late to close the gate or check the advance. Returning to the stockade, where Turkish troops were pouring through the walls, Constantine — who knew that his empire was lost — made a last, vain attempt to rally his people. Exclaiming, "The city is taken and I am still alive," he dismounted, tore off his imperial insignia, plunged headlong into the oncoming Janissaries — and was never seen again, alive or dead. "The prudent despair of Constantine," as Gibbon describes it, "cast away the purple; amidst the tumult he fell by an unknown hand and his body was buried under a mountain of the

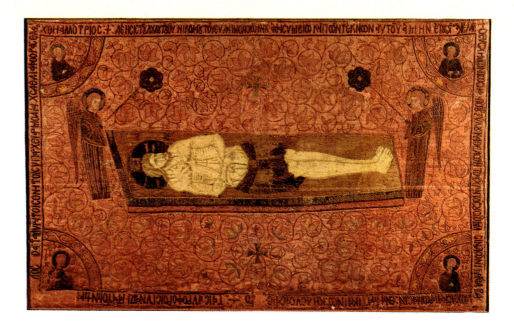

The manuscript illumination at left shows Mohammed II and his attendants riding jubilantly in the Hippodrome after the conquest of Constantinople. Their victory marked the end of the glorious Byzantine artistic tradition that produced such superb works as the embroidered silk shroud at right.

slain." The historian concedes to the emperor a worthy epitaph: "The distress and fall of the last Constantine are more glorious than the long prosperity of the Byzantine Caesars."

After a disciplined march into the city, the conquering soldiery broke ranks and swarmed through the streets in the orgy of slaughter and pillage to which custom entitled them. They sacked churches, monasteries, and convents. They plundered palaces and houses, carrying off not merely their contents but their inhabitants. With the sailors from the harbor they converged on Hagia Sophia, which had been filling with worshipers all night long. The Turks arrived while the faithful were celebrating the service of matins, praying for a miracle to save them. According to the historian Ducas, the unarmed Greeks threw themselves upon the mercy of an angel:

> And in an hour the whole huge sanctuary was full of men and women, below, above, and in the surrounding halls — everywhere — an immeasurable multitude. And shutting the gate, they stood there fervently hoping for deliverance by the angel. Then — fighting all about, killing, taking prisoners — the Turks came to the church, when the first hour of the day was not yet flown. And where they found the doors shut, they battered these in with axes, without compunction.

Some of the older worshipers were killed; most of the rest were tied together with veils and scarves torn from the women and used as ropes. Thus bound, they were herded like slaves to the bivouacs of the soldiers, who quarreled fiercely for possession of the comelier girls, handsomer youths, and more richly clothed senators. The priests continued to chant at the altar until

they too were captured. A few of them — so legend relates — took the holiest vessels and miraculously passed through the south wall of the sanctuary, which opened to admit them and closed behind them. There, walled-up, they are believed to remain to this day, destined to emerge only when Hagia Sophia becomes a Christian church once more.

During the sack that followed, holy vessels were ripped apart or dashed to pieces, while others were simply pocketed whole. Holy icons were stripped of their gold and gems, trampled upon, and then used as seats and tables. Gold-threaded vestments were made into horses' blankets. Reliquaries were opened and their contents defiled. The desecration of Hagia Sophia following the Ottoman conquest led the historian Phrantzes to lament:

> How unfathomable and incomprehensible is Thy wise judgment, O King Christ! We saw the beautiful cathedral of the Holy Wisdom, that heaven on earth, throne of the loveliest of God, seat of the Cherubim, the second citadel of Heaven, creation of the hands of God, the marvellous miracle, the pride of the whole earth, beautiful and more than beautiful — this we looked upon, as the heathens in the holy place ate and drank on the holy altar table and gave free rein to their appetites. Who would not have mourned for you, O holy temple!

Thus, after a lifetime of 1,123 years and a siege of fifty-three days, the Christian city of Constantinople came to an end. On that unlucky Tuesday — a day of the week still shunned by Greeks for any Christian celebration — a twenty-three-year-old Islamic sultan fell heir to the ancient capital of the Roman Empire.

VI
Hagia Sophia as a Mosque

Sultan Mohammed II delayed his own triumphal entry into Constantinople until late afternoon on the day of the conquest, May 29, 1453. Then, escorted by his bodyguard of Janissaries and followed by his ministers, he rode slowly through the streets to the church of Hagia Sophia. Dismounting on the threshold, the sultan bent down and scooped up a handful of earth, which he poured over his turbaned head as an act of humility to his God. Entering the church, he stood still for some moments, gazing silently before him, and then walked toward the altar. As he did so he noticed a Turkish soldier hacking at a piece of the marble pavement. The sultan turned on him, demanding to know why he was destroying the floor. The soldier answered, "For the sake of the Faith." Enraged, Mohammed struck the Turk with his sword, exclaiming, "For you the treasure and the prisoners are enough. The buildings of the city fall to me." According to the Christian historian Ducas, "the Turk was dragged by the feet and thrown outside, half dead."

A few Greeks whom the Turkish soldiery had not captured and bound were still crouching in corners of the church when the sultan entered, and he ordered that they be allowed to depart in peace. A few priests emerged from the secret passages behind the altar and begged him for mercy; they too were sent away under his protection. The sultan then gave orders that the great church be transformed immediately into a mosque. An *ulama,* or Islamic theologian, climbed into the ambo and recited a Moslem prayer, and Mohammed himself mounted the steps of the altar and did obeisance to Allah, the One God, who had brought him his great victory.

Emerging from the building, Mohammed rode across the square to the ruined imperial palace. The streets were quiet as he rode back to his camp. Order was restored. A day's looting had been sufficient reward for the soldiery, and it was time to share the spoils. The extent of the plunder and destruction was great, but it paled before the ravages wrought by the Crusaders 250 years earlier, particularly in Hagia Sophia itself.

On Friday of the first week of the conquest, the people of the city — which would henceforth be known as Istanbul, a Greek name meaning "into the City" — were called to prayer not by a peal of bells but by the cry of the *muezzin.* Consecrated to Moslem worship, the great church was from the outset treated with respect by the conqueror, who retained its name in Islamic form, calling it "the Great Mosque of Aya Sofya." Nor was it deprived of its essential sacred character. As the devout Moslem historian Sa'd-ud-Din observed a century later:

> This ancient building was lit with the sweet-smelling breath of the Law. The hearts of those who bear witness to the Single Nature of God rejoiced at the erection of the True Symbol of the Faith, and this most desirable place of Holiness, this sublime mosque, this temple that quickens the breath, filled with the people of Islam. And the rapture-reflecting interior, illuminated by the proclamation of Unity, began to flash like a polished mirror.

The conqueror supplanted the large metal cross that crowned the summit of the dome with a crescent. This was replaced in the sixteenth century with a larger and more handsome crescent of bronze, said to have

been gilded with 50,000 pieces of gold and to be visible a hundred miles out to sea. Mohammed also removed the ambo, the iconostasis, the thrones, the altar, and all portable icons. Despite the Moslem prohibition on any representation of the human form, he did preserve many Christian figural mosaics, including the figures of the Virgin and Child in the apse. Moreover, he kept many of them free of the whitewash that was to conceal them as time went by. He erected a pulpit in place of the ambo and a *mihrab,* or prayer-niche, in the curve of the sanctuary apse, tilting the axis of worship southeastward, in the direction of Mecca.

Immediately after the conquest a provisional wooden minaret was erected in the southeast corner of the building. Later Mohammed replaced this with a polygonal minaret of brick — the first to be erected in Istanbul and, as such, revered by the Turks as the earliest symbol of the conquest. Its substantial double buttress of stone was built to serve not only as a base for the minaret but, like other such buttresses, as a support for the structure of the building. Three other minarets were added to the mosque in the following century by Mohammed's successors. One of them, fluted and decorated, was added to the northwest corner by Selim II. The other two, one on either side of the west façade, were commissioned during Selim's reign but finished under Murad III. Graceful architectural creations, they serve to frame the somewhat irregular mass of the building.

Hagia Sophia was the only Christian church to be converted into a mosque on the conqueror's official orders. Elsewhere in the city churches were ransacked and desecrated following the siege. In return for the submission of their various parishes, others were spared and continued to be used for Christian worship. It was only with the passage of time that most of the older surviving churches became mosques, while the Christians took to worshiping in newer and less obtrusive buildings.

After the conquest Sultan Mohammed was quick to provide for his Christian subjects, for he saw himself as heir to their emperors and hence responsible for their welfare and that of the Orthodox Church. One of his first tasks was to appoint a new patriarch to replace Gregory Mammas, who had fled the city before its fall. His choice fell upon Gennadius II, leader of those opposed to union between the two churches, who had been captured in his cell at the monastery of the Pantocrator and borne off by the Turks as a slave. Formally elected by a Holy Synod formed from among available bishops, Gennadius was made constitutionally responsible for the good behavior of the Greeks who lived in the *millet,* a self-governing community designed, on a familiar Islamic pattern, for subjects of other creeds that dwelt within the empire.

Early in 1454, Gennadius was invested with the insignia of his office, including a new and splendid pectoral cross that was given him by the sultan. The ceremony was performed in the Church of the Holy Apostles, which Mohammed had spared from destruction to serve as the patriarchal church, the role played by Hagia Sophia before its conversion into a mosque. Gennadius rode to the church on a white horse, also given him by the sultan, who blessed his new patriarch with the words: "Be patriarch, with good fortune, and be assured of our friendship, keeping all the privileges

Immediately after the Turkish conquest, Hagia Sophia was converted to Moslem worship. Among the alterations ordered by Mohammed II — seen at left in an uncharacteristically benign pose — was the partial removal of such Christian symbols as the crosses that formerly decorated the doors of the structure. Traces of the original crosspieces can still be detected on the door panels below.

that the patriarchs before you enjoyed." It became in effect a friendship, and was sealed by discussions of theology between the two religious leaders.

Some years later the patriarch moved his clergy, followers, treasures, and relics from this predominantly Turkish neighborhood to a quarter close to the Phanar, by the Golden Horn, taking over as his church the convent of the Pammakaristos and gathering around him a secular community that was predominantly Greek. The Church of the Holy Apostles was then demolished, and its site, together with many of its materials, was used by the Greek architect Christodoulos in constructing the conqueror's own tomb and mosque. The building became known as the Mosque of Fatih, the name by which the conqueror's people commonly called him. It was the sultan's boast that, with its external precincts, the Fatih surpassed Hagia Sophia in its total dimensions. As a reward for his work the architect was granted the Church of the Virgin Mouchliotissa and its neighboring streets.

Crowning the westerly crest of the ridge between the Sea of Marmara and the Golden Horn, the Fatih was the first of a succession of great mosques that soon gave a new skyline to the city of Istanbul. The conquest of the city proved to be the dawn of a new age of Turkish architecture — one which owed its inspiration less to the style of the Persians, as the previous Ottoman capital of Bursa had, than to the style of the Byzantines. It was the Christian church of Hagia Sophia, crowning the easterly crest of the ridge, which in its scale and domed construction served as a prototype for the new Moslem places of worship.

No domed building of such dimensions had been

erected for close to a thousand years, partly owing to the decline in Byzantine financial resources after the time of Justinian. But the Ottoman Turks, with their expanding empire, had brought new life and fortune to Istanbul. They could afford, after conquering the city, to build as splendidly as the Greeks had done at the peak of their prosperity. Animated by an inventive artistic spirit and determined to create a new Islamic capital that would surpass that of the Christians, they began to erect buildings in the grand imperial manner. A people with a talent for adopting and adapting the arts of those they conquered, the Turks revived — with new techniques and for new purposes — the form of the mighty dome on the square that had been born with Justinian. They combined it with Islamic elements with which they were already familiar, and adapted the whole to create, within the old walls of Constantinople, a new city of domes punctuated by minarets.

In doing so they were fortunate to be able to call upon the great sixteenth-century architect named Sinan. A near-contemporary of Michelangelo and the acknowledged "father of Ottoman architecture," Sinan enriched his country — and particularly its capital — with hundreds of buildings, both religious and secular, on a spacious and imposing scale. A Janissary — by training a military engineer who had built a number of notable bridges — Sinan was in essence a down-to-earth, practical architect who achieved in all his works a fine order and symmetry. Unlike the Byzantines, he was concerned as much with the external as with the internal design of religious buildings. If his mosques did not quite attain the perfection of the interior of

Hagia Sophia, they did achieve in a more matter-of-fact fashion a combination of simplicity with grace and lightness with strength that is distinctively Turkish.

Sinan's imperial patron was Sultan Suleiman the Magnificent — known to his people as Suleiman the Lawgiver — to whom he became architect in chief. It was only after a long career in the sultan's army that Sinan turned, at the age of fifty, to the design of full-scale works of architecture. Supplied by his sovereign with the means and the impetus to employ a large atelier of apprentices and craftsmen, he built three imperial mosques for members of Suleiman's family — the Sehzade for the sultan's favorite son; the Mihrimah for his sister; and finally, just a century after the conquest, the great Suleimaniye for the sultan himself.

The Greek architect who designed the conqueror's mosque had roofed and vaulted it in a manner similar to that of Hagia Sophia — perhaps because Mohammed II liked the wide-open expanse of the great church's central floor space and, after its conversion, found it appropriate for Moslem prayer. The Beyazid mosque, designed and built by another architect early in the sixteenth century, embodied forms similar to those of Hagia Sophia but with different spatial effects. Sinan himself had made a profound and detailed study of the plan of Hagia Sophia, and in designing his earlier buildings he had experimented with ideas for its adaptation to Moslem ritual uses. Hagia Sophia stood out on the city's acropolis as a challenge to any architect, and Sinan rose to it in the Suleimaniye, a building inspired by the ground plan of the great church but of necessity different in both function and design (see Guide to the Mosques of Istanbul, page 164).

LA SOLIMANIE · BASTIE PAR · SVLTAN SOLIMAN

The mosques that were built in the years following the conquest transformed the appearance of the former Byzantine capital. In the late seventeenth century, the French traveler and artist G. J. Grelot sketched the Suleimaniye (near left), the imperial mosque of Sultan Suleiman the Magnificent. Grelot's drawing of Hagia Sophia (far left) clearly reveals the four Moslem minarets added at the corners.

From his intimate knowledge of Hagia Sophia, Sinan was well qualified to supervise certain works of restoration that it came to require in the sixteenth century. The erection of later buildings, including a government warehouse, around the original structure may have weakened its foundations. In any event, the mosque appeared to be in imminent danger of collapsing. After Sultan Selim III examined Hagia Sophia in person in 1573, he instructed Sinan — who retained the post of chief architect that had been conferred upon him by Selim's father, Suleiman — to pull down the excrescent buildings and render the mosque secure. This Sinan did, leaving a space for its reinforcement with new buttresses and sustaining pillars, which were to be built from the stones thus made available.

At the same time the supporting walls of one of the large pyramidal buttresses built by Emperor Andronicus were raised and consolidated. Later other buttresses were reinforced where the structure appeared to demand it. Meanwhile Sinan designed and built, for two successive sultans, the remaining two minarets. He also carried out extensive internal and external repairs.

By the seventeenth century the interior of Hagia Sophia was equipped with all the internal structures and furnishings customary in a mosque of its size and importance. In the reign of Murad IV, four tribunes, or railed balconies, were built below the piers by the eastern apse. The largest of these was oriented in the direction of Mecca, and readings of the Koran were conducted from all four. There was also a sultan's box, which Ahmed III replaced with another in the eighteenth century. The preacher ascending it would carry in one hand a Koran and in the other a wooden sword, a custom observed in captured cities where churches had been turned into mosques. Two flags in the sacred Moslem colors, green embroidered with gold, hung from the pulpit as symbols of the victory of Islam over Christianity and Judaism, and of the Koran over the Old and New Testaments.

Flanking the *mihrab* were two colossal candles on inverted columnar bases that were brought as spoils of war from Hungary and installed by Sultan Suleiman. Hanging from the piers, and from the shafts of columns, were frames containing texts from Moslem scripture. One of these, on the southerly pier, read, "Haste ye to prayer ere the other hath passed"; the other, to the north, read, "Haste ye to repentance ere death cometh."

At the western end of the mosque, standing at the foot of the porphyry columns on either side of the central door that leads into the narthex, were two large alabaster urns, installed by Murad III for the ablutions of the faithful. Hellenistic or Roman in style, they are said to have been unearthed, full of gold, with another, by a peasant plowing near Pergamum. According to popular tradition, he promptly reburied them and went to Istanbul to relate his discovery to the sultan. By the sultan's orders, two of the urns were removed and the third was presented to the peasant. Before accepting it, he required it to be emptied, explaining to the vizier, "Our sultan gave me the urn. He said nothing about the gold it contained." As a further reward for his honesty the peasant was presented with the field in which the urns were found.

Since Hagia Sophia became a mosque a number of

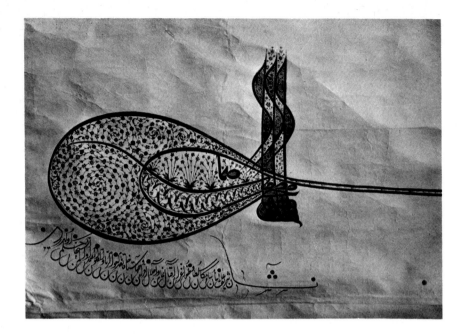

Suleiman the Magnificent, the greatest Ottoman sultan of the sixteenth century, appears at right as a wise old man attended by two swordsmen. The striking design at left is, in fact, Suleiman's signature, as it was executed by a court calligrapher on official documents.

Moslem buildings have sprung up in its precincts. The conqueror himself attached several *medresses,* or theological schools, to the mosque, and a professorial chair at Hagia Sophia became a distinction much coveted by Islamic scholars. The mosque also acquired a notable library. Among the buildings that still survive to the southeast of the main structure are the octagonal or hexagonal tombs of three Ottoman sultans — Mohammed II, Selim II, and Murad III — with their wives and families.

A further mausoleum is the former baptistery of the church, which was used after the capture of the city in 1453 as an oil storehouse and then, in the early seventeenth century, as a tomb for the lunatic Mustafa I and his nephew Sultan Ibrahim. In the course of time, other sarcophagi were added. Interred in these tombs are the remains of five sultans, three sultanas, and 140 royal children, all of whom died within three-quarters of a century (1574–1648), when life in the Ottoman imperial family was cheap. On his accession at the end of the sixteenth century, for instance, Sultan Mohammed III put his nineteen brothers to death — and then celebrated their passing and that of their father, Murad III, with funeral rites of great pomp and solemnity. When Mohammed himself died after a short reign, an inscription was placed above his tomb which reads: "Almighty Allah hath said everything perisheth except mercy and judgment, and they return to thee."

To the west of these tombs is an octagonal fountain of ablutions erected in the eighteenth century by Sultan Mahmud I. Decorative in style, it rests on slender marble columns and pointed arches. Beyond it, at the northwestern angle of the mosque, is a group of low, domed buildings, built as an *imaret,* or almshouse, together with cells for the Moslem clergy.

A full account of the mosque of Hagia Sophia at this time is given by Evliya Chelebi, a seventeenth-century Turkish traveler and writer who numbered among his forebears a standard-bearer at the conquest of Constantinople. As a young man with a melodious voice, Evliya had mastered the art of reading the whole of the Koran in one of seven different modes in seven hours, and he had actually performed the duty of *muezzin* at Hagia Sophia. There he had attracted the attention and the patronage of Sultan Murad IV, who took great delight in the incomparable mosque. According to Evliya, when Murad went to Friday prayers he "caused cages, containing a great number of singing birds, and particularly nightingales, to be hung up there, so that their sweet notes, mingled with the tones of the muezzins' voices, filled the mosque with a harmony approaching to that of Paradise."

He describes, as worshipers at the church had done before, the brilliance of its lighting. During the month-long Fast of Ramadan, two thousand wax tapers perfumed with camphor flickered inside the building. According to Evliya, those lamps "pour forth streams of light upon light; and in the center of the dome a circle of lamps represents in letters . . . that text of the Scripture, 'God is the light of the heavens and the earth.'" Comparing Hagia Sophia to the great mosques of Jerusalem, Damascus, and Cairo, he observes that "it is always full of holy men, who pass the day there in fasting and the night in prayer. Seventy lectures (on theology) well pleasing to God

During the eighteenth and nineteenth centuries, foreign architectural experts flocked to Constantinople — renamed Istanbul by the Turks — to study its most intriguing edifice, Hagia Sophia. The sketch at left of the interior is by a Swedish engineer, Cornelius Loos; the ground plan below and the façade at right were drawn by Charles Texier, a French scholar and traveler.

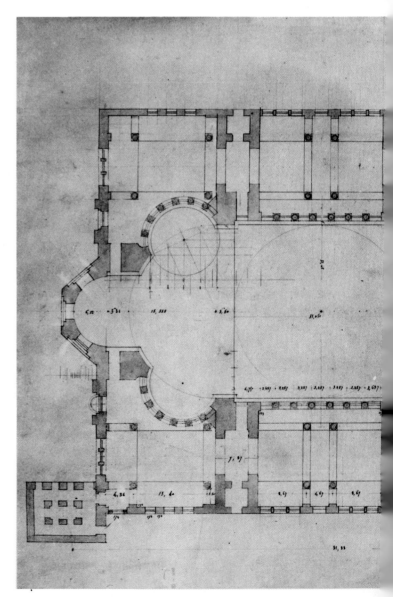

are delivered there daily, so that to the student it is a mine of knowledge, and it never fails to be full of multitudes every day."

At this time the mosque of Hagia Sophia — apart from the narthex — was closed to non-Moslems except by the special favor of a *firman,* or edict, from the sultan. As Busbecq, the ambassador from Austria to Turkey in the sixteenth century, explains in a letter, "the Turks hold that the entrance of a Christian profanes their places of worship."

The practice of purveying tesserae from the gold mosaic backgrounds to tourists became an established trade in the 1800's. At the end of the century, James Dallaway described a chapel "with a vault of mosaic almost destroyed . . . sold in small fragments to the superstitious Greeks, or curious visitors, by the inferior officials of the mosque." With regard to the figural mosaics of Hagia Sophia, it seems certain enough that after the conquest only those within easy reach of the floor were covered with plaster or whitewash by the Turks. As a general rule those less easily accessible — that is to say the majority — remained exposed for some three centuries, though eyes were sometimes put out, noses destroyed, and faces otherwise disfigured in a haphazard fashion. Evliya describes the four "archangels" in the pendentives supporting the dome; at a later date their faces were obliterated.

It may have been Sinan, in the course of his restorations in the sixteenth century, who covered up the mosaics in the tympana. It seems that the face of the Pantocrator, in the main dome, was obscured before 1630 or earlier, but that the figure remained visible for some time longer. The mosaic of the Virgin and

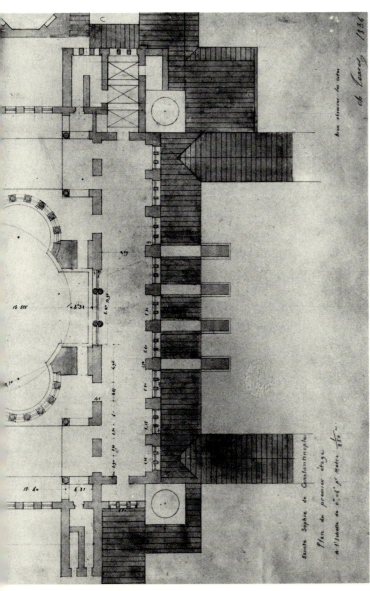

Child in the apse was still there in 1672 when the French traveler and artist G. F. Grelot commented: "It should be a good augury for the Christians that, thanks to a Divine Providence, the images which covered the Holy of Holies of this church have remained intact until this day, although they are in quite a frequented spot, which can easily be reached."

Grelot's drawings and plans provided scholars and visitors with an accurate description of Hagia Sophia until the middle of the nineteenth century, and it was presumably on these that Gibbon based his dry, eighteenth-century view of its exterior:

> The eye of the spectator is disappointed by an irregular prospect of half-domes and shelving roofs: the western front, the principal approach, is destitute of simplicity and magnificence; and the scale of the dimensions has been much surpassed by several of the Latin cathedrals. But the architect who first erected an *aerial* cupola is entitled to the praise of bold design and skillful execution.

The mosaics in the apse, those above the Imperial Door, and those in the vaults of the north and south galleries, were still visible in the early eighteenth century at the time when King Charles XII of Sweden visited the great mosque. In fact, the mosaics were depicted in 1710 by the Swedish engineer Cornelius Loos in drawings still on display in the Stockholm Museum. In 1738 Lord Sandwich wrote that the dome was adorned with a "Gothic mosaic," as were the walls of the mosque. Saints, crosses, and other symbols of the Christian religion were thus represented, and these the Turks had endeavored to repair by painting them to match the surviving portions. But after the

By the middle of the nineteenth century, natural disasters and human neglect had combined to make the restoration of Hagia Sophia imperative. In 1846 Sultan Abdul Medjid commissioned two Swiss architects, Gaspare and Giuseppe Fossati, to undertake the monumental assignment. The Fossati engraving of the sunlit interior at left minimizes its shabby and dilapidated condition. In order to shore up the exterior walls of the mosque, the brothers first had to demolish the auxiliary buildings (overleaf) that surrounded it.

middle of the eighteenth century the remaining mosaics were systematically covered with a crust of limewash, leaving only the headless seraphim in the pendentives. Curiously enough, although the mosaics remained uncovered and were seen by numerous European visitors until a relatively late date, few travelers' accounts of them survive. This may be due to the fact that a true interest in Byzantine painting and decoration did not awaken in Europe until the nineteenth century — and by that time the mosaics were no longer visible.

Structurally, the mosque of Hagia Sophia had fallen into a state of disrepair by the end of the eighteenth century. No major repairs had been undertaken since those supervised by Sinan two centuries earlier. A series of earthquake shocks in 1766 did some damage to the building, but a subsequent shock in 1802 seems to have left it undamaged. Its dilapidated condition was thus due not to any natural calamity but to persistent human neglect. Early in the nineteenth century it seems that some restoration was carried out by a pasha who had formerly held the post of chief butcher to the sultan, and in the course of his work many slabs of marble revetment were either broken or stolen. No clear record of this episode exists, however.

Charles Texier, the French scholar and traveler, made a survey of the building in 1834 but met with obstacles in getting permission to work there. In the following year a Russian architect named Efimov made a superficial, five-day survey of the building in which he incorporated a design for the restoration of the western façade, fancifully inspired by that of Saint Mark's in Venice. Some years earlier the Reverend Robert Walsh,

chaplain to the British Embassy in Istanbul, recorded that a severe storm had caused one of the smaller domes to fall into the church. "On clearing away the surface of rubbish," he wrote, "the flooring was found covered with glittering cubes which had formed the ceiling, and, in such abundance, that everyone was supplied with as much as he chose to take for a trifling gratuity."

During this period, the Ottoman Empire embarked on a policy of liberal reforms that led to an era of increasing Westernization. In 1839 a young reforming sultan named Abdul Medjid issued an imperial edict, the Hatt-I Sherif of Gulhané, designed to eliminate all discrimination on the grounds of race, creed, and nationality in his empire. This brought a new influx of Europeans and European ideas into Istanbul. The process of Westernization was exemplified by the encouragement of European architecture by government, the pashas, and an expanding mercantile class. This led to a general boom in Westernized building, particularly in the new quarter of Pera, perched opposite the old city, above Galata and to the north of the Golden Horn, Istanbul's fabled harbor.

Foreign powers, in a spirit of rivalry, built new embassies in a cumbrous neoclassical style with some Oriental decorative motifs. The first to arise in Pera was the British; the second was the Russian embassy, a vast and substantial pile on the crest of the hill. This building attracted the young sultan's special attention. Its designers were two Swiss brothers, Gaspare and Giuseppe Fossati, who had received architectural training in Milan and who assembled in Istanbul a large force of technicians and skilled labor from Russia and Italy. They were promptly taken into the service of

the Ottoman government, for whom they erected a number of buildings. In 1846 the sultan gave them a new and challenging commission: to undertake the full restoration of Hagia Sophia. Recent, routine repairs had made the need for this evident by revealing the mosque's dilapidated condition. Gaspare Fossati wrote that "already the vaults and the cracked domes were letting in the rain, the wind, and the snow." He went on to condemn "the negligence of the Moslem officials responsible for the conservation of the building, who even omitted to repair the lead roofs, allowed the whole building to be invaded, within and without, by clouds of pigeons and destructive birds of prey; in a word, everything was tending toward the imminent ruin of Santa Sophia."

In employing Christians to do the repair work, the sultan inevitably aroused opposition from reactionary Moslem elements. In launching the work he thus took advantage of the departure of the annual pilgrimage to Mecca, encouraging the more fanatical *imams* of the mosque to proceed there. The restoration was financed by a legacy from a childless sheikh, and its ultimate total cost amounted to the equivalent of $1,500,000. Work began in May 1847, with a force of eight hundred laborers — an inconveniently large number, engaged to satisfy the claims of competing contractors. An immense scaffolding was erected, and Fossati was pleased to record that only two workmen fell to their deaths from it, while a third escaped with nothing worse than a broken arm. One of the dead men was a Christian, and it is related that as he lay dying fellow workmen brought in a priest who secretly and hurriedly administered the last rites to him — probably the

first Christian prayers to be uttered in the mosque of Hagia Sophia.

Fossati's work fell into three successive categories: consolidation, redecoration, and the erection of new structures. First he straightened thirteen columns in the gallery whose inclination had alarmed visitors for some time. According to his calculation, they had "deviated more than half a foot from the perpendicular." He rectified this by removing the original base of each column, shifting the shaft to its upright position, then inserting a new base beneath it. Even so, one of the columns at the southeastern angle of the church still inclines at an angle of seven degrees from the vertical. The columns affected were in the *exedrae,* and Fossati believed that their inclination had been caused by the outward thrust of the two lateral arches supporting the dome on the north and south sides. His remedy for this was to reinforce these arches with tie rods. To further relieve the thrust, he removed the two staircase turrets at the eastern corners of the dome's base.

To fortify the dome itself — in which cracks had appeared following earthquakes — Fossati bound it with two iron chains, one around the foot of the hemisphere and the other, concealed by a plaster cornice, around the square base. Having done so, he removed the four flying buttresses that had been added to the north and south sides of the dome after its first fall in the sixth century, since he believed they were of no further structural importance. He repaired the lead roofs, and he cleared from the four main buttresses the debris left in them from earlier repairs.

When it came to redecoration, Fossati was primarily concerned with the marble revetments, to which he

In the Fossati view below, groups of Moslem worshipers squat on prayer rugs beneath the hulking arches of the refurbished nave of Hagia Sophia — whose polished revetments, fresh plaster, and repainted stucco sparkle with renewed luster.

applied new cramps and fresh cement. No new marble was introduced: slabs missing from the walls were replaced by others taken from the pavement or imitated in painted stucco to harmonize with the original patterns and coloring. As the work drew to an end, the revetments were polished to remove accumulated dirt and to revive some of their former brilliance.

What Fossati had not foreseen in his plans for restoration was the extent to which he would be required to uncover the original mosaics. This was to prove the major work in his redecoration — a heavy responsibility for one who was more architect than artist by training and temperament. He found mosaics for the first time while working on the vaults of the north aisle. Fossati covered them with a veil and then invited the sultan to inspect them. When he removed the veil, the sultan was so amazed to see a vault thus covered with gold that he is said to have exclaimed, "Wretched man, you have ruined me!" When the Swiss architect explained that this was not his own work but that of past generations, the sultan criticized his own forebears for their concealment of such beautiful ornaments.

After exposing the mosaics and sketching them, Fossati covered them once again, this time with paint, gold leaf, or plaster of an unfortunate ocher shade that has not improved with age. It was said that Fossati himself recommended this course to the sultan, pointing out that certain workmen had already torn the eyes out of a mosaic head. There was clearly a risk of further defacement if these Christian works of art were not concealed from Moslem eyes. In an en-

lightened spirit worthy of his imperial ancestor Mohammed the Conqueror, Abdul Medjid insisted that they be covered in such a way as to make them easy to uncover if ever the time became ripe. He even proposed that the two mosaic groups over the doors in the narthex and vestibule be left exposed, since they were outside the place of prayer. But in the end more reactionary influences prevailed, and they were covered up with the rest.

None of these mosaics was left exposed to view for long. After being described and copied, sometimes sketchily and in haste, they were quickly recovered. In the case of decorative as opposed to figural mosaics, all gaps were filled with plaster and then painted through a stencil to repeat the existing patterns. This work was done, not always sensitively, by an Italian painter named Antonio Fornari who also carried out the false marbling for the revetments.

Completing his redecoration, Fossati renewed the stucco friezes on the ground floor and in the gallery; provided a number of candelabra cast in bronze by a Turkish craftsman; installed three stained-glass windows in the apse; made new wooden doors for the inner narthex; gilded the *minbar*, the *mihrab*, and the tribunes; provided floor rugs, mats, and door curtains; and added a Koranic inscription around the dome that reads: "In the name of God the Merciful and Pitiful. God is the light of heaven and earth. His light is Himself, not as that which shines through glass or gleams in the morning star, or glows in the firebrand."

Fossati also installed eight green placards inscribed with the names of Allah and the prophets high upon the piers. (These enormous disks, each twenty-five feet

*During the course of his restorations, Gaspare
Fossati replaced the old sultan's box — which had
been erected by Ahmed III in the eighteenth
century — with the hexagonal marble one at left.*

in diameter, deface and distort the architectural forms and proportions of Hagia Sophia today.) Finally, he plastered and painted the external walls with red and yellow stripes in the belief that this would give the building "a lighter aspect."

Within the building, Fossati removed the old sultan's box and replaced it with a new one designed in an ornate and sumptuous style that he believed was Byzantine. Built of marble and placed against a pier, it stands on six columns, three of which were found in the courtyard of the conqueror's mosque. Its balustrade is an elaborate gilded grille, and a flamboyant gilded sunburst crowns its hexagonal roof. The box connects by means of a raised passage with a *salon* designed in Fossati's version of the "purest Greco-Roman style" and decorated by Fornari with views of Medina and Mecca. A marble slab adorned with a mosaic *tughra,* the sultan's signature seal, was added to the interior of the box by another Italian artist. Among external structures, Fossati built the clock-house, a small square building within the courtyard gate. He also heightened the brick minaret that was built by Mohammed II to raise it to the level of the other three, adding a frieze of festoons beneath its conical roof.

Restored over a period of two years, Hagia Sophia was inaugurated with ceremonial splendor on July 13, 1849, by the young sultan, his court officials, and his religious chiefs. At midday, as salvos of gunfire echoed from both sides of the Bosporus, Abdul Medjid emerged from his palace riding a white horse decked with a gilded and pearl-studded harness. Passing through the great gate of his seraglio, he entered the square before Hagia Sophia. Clad in his finest official array — a diamond-collared cloak with the plumed imperial aigrette crowning his forehead — he rode with his grand vizier to the church, followed respectfully on foot by a cortege of court dignitaries, while a band played appropriate music outside the gate. Outside, his mother, Sultana Valide, sat in a gilded coach drawn by four horses. Inside, the sultan's children, his brother, and his entire harem watched the procession as it passed.

On the threshold of the great mosque, the sultan was received by the *ulamas* and the brothers Fossati. In the course of the Islamic liturgy that followed, the building was reconsecrated by the Sheikh of Islam, the grand mufti, and the attendant high clergy. Prayers were then recited for the prosperity of the state and the well-being of the all-powerful, all-merciful sultan who had initiated this great work of homage to the god of the Prophet Mohammed. The sultan himself graciously thanked the two architects in his own name and that of his people for having restored the beautiful mosque, "quite different to what it was yesterday, but just as in principle it should have been."

The sultan then retired to the salon adjoining his box, where he gazed with approval upon Fornari's frescoes of Mecca and Medina and paid the artist a felicitous compliment: "You enable me to make the holy pilgrimage, which, as ruler of the empire I can only do by proxy. I thank you." That night the ceremonies reached a climax with illuminations, fireworks, and "delights of all kinds." A commemorative medal, showing Hagia Sophia on one side and the sultan's *tughra* on the other, had been ordered in Paris,

Among the many Moslem additions to Justinian's former church are two alabaster urns (one is visible at right) used for ablutions by the faithful.

but was not ready in time for the occasion.

Such was the last major restoration of Hagia Sophia. The building was to be struck by one more earthquake, in the summer of 1894. But its structure was not seriously affected, and no sign of a crack disfigures its outer walls. The interior decoration — notably the plaster revetment — was damaged, however, and this necessitated the closing of the mosque for repairs. The affected areas were then replastered in a lighter shade than before.

More serious was the damage done to certain mosaics in the western arch, notably a head of the Virgin and the fragmentary figures of Saint Peter and Saint Paul. Fossati had uncovered the latter two, but they had disappeared in the course of replastering. Other mosaics may indeed have vanished as a result of the 1894 earthquake, for Fossati's workmen seem to have destroyed none but a few — and those were already in a very precarious condition.

Ceremonial processions to Hagia Sophia took place each year at the Feast of Bairam that ended the Fast of Ramadan. Their Oriental splendors attracted the curious and often admiring attention of the European visitors who now thronged Istanbul. Although impressed by the procession, they did not always agree in their admiration of the mosque itself. Gustave Flaubert, visiting Hagia Sophia the year after its restoration, found its exterior "a graceless amalgam of buildings, with ponderous minarets," but he was impressed by the interior. Looking down from above, he noted that the chandeliers seemed "as though they were touching the ground, and one does not see how men can pass beneath them." The poet Lamartine, on the other hand, visited this "Rome of the East" and conceded that the dome was as majestic as that of Saint Peter's itself. Otherwise he saw only "in the barbarism of the art which inspired this mass of stone, that it was the work of an age of corruption and decadence. It is the confused, coarse relic of a taste which is no more; it is the rough, formless skeleton of an art which experiments." The Turkish mosques of the city he found less vast but infinitely more beautiful.

In 1881, Lady Dufferin, wife of the British Ambassador, admired the interior of the building — although like most other visitors she deplored the inscribed wooden shields at the corners as "not worthy of the marble columns and beautiful architecture." The evening Ramadan service she described as "one of the grandest things I ever saw." Arriving early with the ambassadorial party, she gazed down from a gallery upon the immense inner chamber where she saw "children rushing about, shrieking and thoroughly enjoying their enormous playground."

An earlier English visitor, Lord Carlisle, stood beneath the dome and imagined that he could see "the great portals thrown open, and the long procession of priests advance, with miter, and banner, and crucifix, and clouds of incense, and blaze of torches, and bursts of harmony, and lustral sprinklings, and low prostrations." He added, with a touch of overoptimism, "It may not, however, be unattainable in the righteous providence of God, that when Christianity reestablishes her own domain here, it shall be with the blessed accompaniments of a finer ritual and more spiritual worship." Hearing the *muezzin's* call, he reflected, "Yes; and how long shall that call continue?"

VII

Hagia Sophia as a Museum

How long indeed? The twentieth century dawned. Its first decades were to witness the fall of the Ottoman Empire, its defeat in war and its dismemberment, and finally the rise from its ashes of the Turkish Republic. This sequence of events began in 1908 when a revolutionary party known as the "Young Turks" rebelled against the thirty-two-year tyranny of Sultan Abdul-Hamid II — Abdul the Damned — and forced him to restore the democratic constitution first proclaimed in 1876 and subsequently abrogated. Its restoration was followed, on December 17, 1908, by the opening of a new Turkish parliament in a hall on the site of the old Byzantine senate house, which had been abandoned for a generation to the nesting pigeons of nearby Hagia Sophia.

On that December day, the space before this stronghold of the faith was filled, in the words of an English observer, G. F. Abbott, "with an ocean of human faces seething and swaying round the flashing blades of many bayonets. Its very roof, buttresses, pillars, cornices, and minarets were flooded with the fezes and turbans of men and the veils of women." A whole nation had gathered together to celebrate the passing of the "days of oppression" and the enthronement of constitutional liberty. George Young, a contemporary historian, saw the whole Hippodrome and the former Augustaeum as "a sea of red fezes, green and white turbans, Albanian Guards in white uniforms, Syrian Zouaves in green turbans, students, clericals, and uniforms of every fashion. There are the red banners, the green banners, and the black banners with silver inscriptions. . . . A long procession of carriages, full of deputies, notables, ladies of the Harem, ecclesiastics and Ambassadors, crawls up to . . . the Parliament."

The procession was blocked for ten minutes by a shepherd boy and his flock on their annual journey from the Anatolian pastures — a journey that antedates Byzantium itself. When the road was cleared, a carriage drawn at a gallop by six white Arabian horses came rumbling up the hill amid the distant cries of the crowd. Seated in it was Sultan Abdul-Hamid, who lived in seclusion behind the high, impregnable walls of Yildiz Palace, across the Golden Horn, and was seldom seen by his people. Presently he appeared at the front of a box in the parliament house, looking, according to Young, like "a hunched, scraggy-bearded, hook-nosed Shylock, in a gray military overcoat with red facings and heavy epaulettes." To one hostile witness he resembled "some treacherous beast of prey, that after hiding in a cave for years is finally trapped, caged, and brought forth, blinking and reluctant, into the blessed sunlight." The sultan read his speech: "I have prompted progress in all parts of my empire. . . ." Prayers followed. Inaudible in the din from the booming of cannon and the cheering of the masses outside, Abdul-Hamid was "understood by his gestures to be calling down the blessings of Allah upon the new regime." Only a few months later, following an abortive counterrevolution, the hapless puppet sultan was deposed by the Young Turks and succeeded on the tottering Ottoman throne by his brother Mohammed V.

Mohammed may have been a somewhat more dynamic leader than his brother had become, but even he was unable to reverse the empire's decline. The tide of conquest was turning from West to East: in 1912 and

122

the following year, the oppressed peoples of the Balkans rose in two successive wars against the Ottoman Empire. Once again there was an iron ring around Istanbul. Most of European Turkey had been lost, and the Bulgarians who had besieged the city were preparing to march into it through the Golden Gate. They were intent upon placing a cross on the dome of Hagia Sophia, which was then serving as a hospital for the victims of a cholera epidemic. The prospect of plunder attracted art dealers from all parts of the world, but disappointment awaited them: the defenses held, internal dissensions divided the enemy powers, and Istanbul was spared.

By 1914 Turkey was at war once again, this time allied with Germany and Austria against England and France. World War I started very badly for the Turks: after severe Turkish reverses in the east, the Allies launched an offensive against Istanbul through the Dardanelles with several troop landings on the Gallipoli Peninsula. The Turkish government made plans to evacuate the city, moving the archives from the Sublime Porte and the gold from its banks across into Anatolia. They buried works of art in the cellars of the city's museums, and even planned to dynamite a number of public buildings, among them Hagia Sophia. When the American ambassador protested that the great monument should be spared, a leading Young Turk replied that there were not six men in his party who cared for anything old. But before the fuses were laid, the Allied offensive collapsed. Once more Istanbul had won a temporary reprieve.

It was not until 1918 that the victorious Allied forces finally entered and occupied the city. The government of the Young Turks resigned, its principal leaders fled into exile, and Sultan Mohammed VI bowed to the will of the Allies. The Greeks swaggered through the streets of Istanbul, jostling the Turks, and a rumor spread through the city: "They are putting the bells into Aya Sofya." Waves of irate Moslems surged up to the mosque — only to discover that Turkish troops were still guarding its courtyard.

Under such circumstances the likelihood of a new revolution grew. In 1919 a young officer named Mustafa Kemal, the hero of Gallipoli and the only Turkish commander without a defeat to his name, emerged as his country's savior. Destined to make his mark as one of the truly great leaders of the twentieth century, Kemal emulated, in a new republican sphere, such giants of the Byzantine and Ottoman empires as Justinian and Mohammed the Conqueror. Like Alexander the Great, Kemal was a Macedonian, born to Turkish middle-class parents in the cosmopolitan port of Salonika. He thus grew up in a world where East mingled with West, Moslem with Christian and Jew, and Turk with Greek, Slav, Vlach, and Albanian. As a young officer Kemal became familiar with the nationalist upsurge, the intense desire to break free of Ottoman imperial rule that gripped Turkey in Europe. He thus saw the East crumbling before the West just as the West had crumbled before the East six centuries earlier. He came to know and understand both worlds at close quarters. Fiercely patriotic in defense of his Turkish fatherland, he was at the same time keenly attuned to the West, with its civilizing influences and the political and cultural benefits its advances could bring to his people.

Silhouetted against a sunset sky, the vertical spires of the minarets and the squat curve of the vast dome evoke Hagia Sophia's ageless grandeur.

To Kemal and the small group of young officers who gathered around him, civilization meant European civilization, and this — as a progressive Turkish writer of the time expressed it — must be imported "with both its roses and its thorns." Together these friends absorbed the works of the philosophers of the French Revolution and discussed its principles of popular sovereignty in relation to their own country's problems. But the declining Ottoman Empire was not yet ready for so radical an approach to democracy. These self-professed "revolutionaries" were in fact little more than liberal-minded reformers; they sought not to destroy the theocratic regime of the sultans but to conserve it within the tempering framework of a liberal constitution. It was not until Turkey's defeat in World War I that the situation seemed to call for a solution as drastic as the true revolution that Mustafa Kemal — with his keen sense of reality and his wider political vision — had been brooding over for the past decade.

Kemal's opportunity had finally come, but it still had no more than an outside chance of success. The Allies continued to occupy the empire, and at the peace conference in Paris they planned not merely to free its outlying Arab and Balkan provinces but to partition the core of Turkey itself — with a zone for the French, a zone for the Italians, and a zone for the Greeks. To achieve this, they counted on the mute collaboration of a puppet sultan, his defeatist government, and a badly demoralized Turkish people. To Mustafa Kemal a loss of the outlying Ottoman provinces meant little. From his youth he had divined that the day of empires was done and the day of nations

125

was at hand. Renouncing all imperialism, he sought to make Turkey great once more by keeping her small. What mattered in his eyes was to save Anatolia, the heart of the old Turkish homeland, and to make of it a new Turkish nation.

Having ascertained that he could count on support from the few loyal officers that he had gathered around him, Kemal contrived to obtain an official posting to Anatolia. On May 19, 1919, he landed on its Black Sea coast and launched a resistance movement directed against both the Allies and the sultan's government. His arrival happened to coincide with a landing staged by Greek forces on the Aegean coast. They started to advance inland, a move that gave Kemal just the spark he needed to ignite popular feeling behind his resistance. To the people of Anatolia, at this time of defeat, the presence on their soil of French or Italian enemy forces might be accepted as a necessary evil. But invasion by the Greeks — rebellious and disloyal subjects for a century past — was an affront not to be borne. Influential groups in the towns and the countryside of Anatolia rallied to support the new leader in his war of Turkish independence.

Kemal at once gave political form to his military resistance by issuing a Declaration of Independence — a statement of war aims. He then summoned two successive congresses, held respectively at Erzurum and at Sivas, whose delegates agreed upon a National Pact. Based on the Allies' own principles of self-determination, the pact insisted upon the preservation of Turkey's existing frontiers, defining them as those which contained a Turkish-speaking majority. It denied privileges to non-Turkish minorities, and allowed for

the election of a provisional Nationalist government. This took concrete form in April 1920 with the inauguration of a Grand National Assembly, the first Kemalist parliament, at Angora. It followed the resignation, under Nationalist pressure, of the sultan's government, and a subsequent raid by the Allies on the Istanbul parliament, which was thus dissolved for the last time.

Such was the start of a revolutionary struggle that was to last more than four weary years. In the course of it, Mustafa Kemal, who had already proven himself as a soldier, had to prove himself as a politician, a diplomat, and finally a statesman. With his erect bearing, his light build, and his clean-cut features, he had the look of the soldier. But there was within him an extra dimension that his companions lacked. It gleamed through his eyes, which were gray and stern and unblinking. Forever fixing, observing, appraising, they reflected a quick, intuitive vision and a determination that enabled him to accomplish his objective. A realist in a land given to dreams and abstractions, he saw that his aims could be achieved only by slow and patient stages. A master both of tactics and timing, he pursued what was possible and postponed what was not, as he advanced step by step toward the goal that he had set for his country. It was a goal that he dared define, at this stage, only by the vague but emotive phrase, "the sovereignty of the people" — a concept of government still unfamiliar in any Eastern country.

Meanwhile, Kemal the soldier was fighting both a foreign war and a civil war against superior forces — the Greeks on the one hand, the sultan's regular and irregular forces on the other. To prevail, he had to

Mustafa Kemal (left), the leader of the nationalist movement that deposed the last of the Ottoman sultans, became the first president of the new Turkish Republic in 1923. He assumed the name Atatürk, "Father of the Turks," instituted a policy of Westernization, and transformed the nation's foremost shrine, Hagia Sophia, into a secular museum.

build up a regular army from scratch, and to produce arms for it he had to create workshops that literally forged plowshares into swords. He evolved a form of total war in which the entire civilian population, male and female, played a part. As his strength grew, he forced the Greeks to retire from the line of the Sakarya River — a mere forty miles from Angora — after one of the longest pitched battles in history. When ready — but not a moment before — his forces drove the invaders into the Aegean Sea in a lightning campaign and took possession of Smyrna.

Kemal the diplomat then bluffed his way, without firing a shot, along the shores of the Straits and through the defended "neutral zone" at Cannakale. There he managed to secure an armistice — prelude to a peace treaty and the reoccupation of Istanbul. In October 1922 his advance representative, Refet Pasha, was rapturously welcomed to the capital, where he addressed a huge congregation from the pulpit of Hagia Sophia, reducing many to tears while others surged forward to kiss his hands and his garments. Soon afterward Kemal, with the Assembly behind him, abolished the sultanate as an instrument of temporal power, retaining only the caliphate, its spiritual counterpart. Thus the last sultan of the Ottoman Empire retired into exile. Finally, on July 24, 1923, the Treaty of Lausanne was signed between the Allies and Turkey. It granted the nation the frontiers and other concessions that it had sought in the National Pact — making it the only treaty signed after World War I in which an enemy obtained its own terms from the Allies.

Angora, soon to be known as Ankara, replaced Istanbul as the capital of Turkey. "The war is over,"

was the saying in Angora, "long live the war." There was to be no resting on the laurels of victory, however. Mustafa Kemal, soon to be known as Atatürk, or "Father of the Turks," had saved and revived his country; he was then faced with the task of remaking it. He launched a new campaign whose objective was nothing less than the transformation of Turkish society and whose principal enemy was the reactionary forces of Islam. The long awaited moment had come to sweep away Turkey's medieval social system, based for centuries on the Moslem religious code, and replace it with a new society based on modern Western civilization. Islam as a way of life and a source of social and political power must no longer be permitted to hold back democracy.

The first step toward this was the proclamation of a Turkish Republic on October 29, 1923, and the election of Atatürk as its first president by the Assembly. The next step, taken a few months later and involving the complete disestablishment of Islam, was the abolition of the caliphate and the departure of the caliph, who followed his cousin the sultan into exile. On the following Friday, the call to prayer that issued from the great mosque of Hagia Sophia omitted all mention of the caliphate: "O God, grant thy protecting aid to our Republican Government and the Moslem nation. Make eternal the glory of the Moslems and raise the flag of Islam, which rests upon the Republic of Turkey, above all other flags and make them live by the Spiritual Prophet."

The Turkish Republic thus became a secular state in which the spiritual was distinctly separated from the temporal power — as are Church and State in the

Western Christian world. The religious schools were transferred to the secular arm, religious courts were closed, and Islamic law — governing such matters of family and personal status as marriage, divorce, and inheritance — was replaced by a civil code on the Western model. The fez, symbol of Islam, was ordered removed from the head of the Turkish male; the veil disappeared from the face of the Turkish female. The dervishes were suppressed; the sacred tombs and other such resorts of superstition were closed. Religion ceased to be a political instrument and became a matter of individual conscience. On this basis the mosques remained open and the faithful continued to worship.

But a new, secular future awaited Hagia Sophia, the great shrine that had successively served Christianity and Islam, God and Allah, for fourteen hundred years. Atatürk was aspiring to create, in his Turkish Republic, a fusion between the civilizations of East and West. The shrine of Hagia Sophia, which had long been a symbol of the conflict between them, was now to symbolize their union. Atatürk decided to convert the shrine into a Byzantine-Ottoman museum.

By this time a team of architectural experts had already surveyed the monument and found its foundations to be sound. They had consolidated one of its piers, encircled the dome with a band of reinforced concrete, and taken precautions against seepage. Later, while Hagia Sophia was still being used as a mosque, American experts were permitted to study, measure, and photograph the interior.

Then, in April 1932, members of the Byzantine Institute of America began the task of uncovering its mosaics. In June of 1931 the Turkish government had given the institute permission to "lay bare and conserve" them, for Atatürk recognized that these mosaics were treasures of Christian art that should be shown to the world without Moslem inhibition or concealment. Thomas Whittemore, who was the founder of the institute, immediately established friendly relations with Atatürk. As he liked to tell the story, "Santa Sophia was a mosque the day I talked to him. The next morning, when I went to the mosque, there was a sign on the door written in Atatürk's own hand. It said: 'The museum is closed for repairs.'" In fact, Hagia Sophia did not officially open as a museum until 1934, when it was placed under the auspices of the Ministry of Education. Certain shops and small buildings close to it were then demolished, and others were repaired to improve its general aspect.

A scholar and an archaeologist, Thomas Whittemore was born at Cambridge, Massachusetts, in 1871. He came from an established New England family, studied at Harvard, and graduated from Tufts University, where he later lectured on English and fine arts. In the course of his career he also lectured at Columbia and New York universities on Byzantine and Coptic art; worked as an archaeologist with the Egypt Exploration Fund on excavations at Tell el-Amarna; and was for a time Keeper of Coins and Seals at the Fogg Museum, with a research fellowship at Harvard.

Traveling extensively as a young man, in Greece, Russia, and the Middle East, Whittemore developed a lifelong interest in Byzantine and Russian art, religion, and history. An Anglican since birth, his religious feelings were such that he felt at home in a church of any Christian creed, and he responded in particular

While repairing the interior of Hagia Sophia in the mid-nineteenth century, the Fossati brothers uncovered many incomparable mosaics — but in deference to Moslem custom they concealed them again with whitewash and stencils. By 1931, when the Turkish Republic granted Thomas Whittemore of the Byzantine Institute of America permission to conserve the mosaics, many had suffered almost irreparable damage. Fortunately, the symbolic mosaic in the vestibule, of Justinian and Constantine proffering gifts to the Virgin (left), had survived intact. The two photographs below show the progressive uncovering of that mosaic from beneath Islamic designs.

to the beauty and mysticism of the Greek Orthodox liturgy, with its fine choral music and its ordinance that brought to life the rich ceremonies of the Byzantine court.

In the course of his travels he paid many visits to Mount Athos, the Holy Mountain, in Greece, and particularly to its three Russian monasteries. Richly endowed by tsarist Russia, they were abruptly deprived of supplies by the 1917 Revolution, and Whittemore, with the financial help of friends, sent them periodic shiploads of such commodities as flour, olive oil, shoe leather, and cloth. Arriving in person, he would be welcomed by the abbots and monks with the honors due only to bishops and royalty, walking from the gate of the monastery to the church up a path strewn with flowers and leaves.

Whittemore and his team of experts worked in Hagia Sophia until the outbreak of World War II, and then resumed work again as soon as hostilities ceased. Their working season lasted for some seven months, from spring until autumn, but ceased in winter when the temperatures inside the building fell too low. The team's main task was to undo the work of the Fossati brothers by revealing the figural mosaics they had concealed between 1847 and 1849 with paint and plaster. In this they briefly had the advice of two master mosaicists from Venice. As the work proceeded they received help from technical assistants recommended by the Deputy Keeper of the Palace of Westminster in London.

Thomas Whittemore was a man with both imaginative understanding and a love of the mosaic medium. In spirit an artist, he was also in essence a craftsman,

129

In the photograph at left three of Whittemore's assistants painstakingly uncover the tenth-century mosaics of Saint John Chrysostom (foreground) and Saint Ignatius Theophorus in the north tympanum of Hagia Sophia. The fully cleaned mosaic (right) reveals the noble figure of Saint John, the fifth-century Patriarch of Constantinople.

and he recruited others who were equally scrupulous in their attention to practical detail. In his own phrase, the mosaics were "cleansed and corroborated, but not subjected to subtraction or addition." The use of liquids for cleaning had been strictly excluded, but the prohibition proved unnecessary. Solvents were not needed to remove paint, which was so thinly spread that it could easily be flaked off with a small steel chisel comparable to those used, as Whittemore put it, "in delicately cleaning fossils and scraping varnish and over-painting from pictures." But the removal of plaster without disturbing the mosaic was harder work and, with the process of strengthening, took longer.

Fossati's hasty and often slapdash methods of restoration — perfunctory stenciling, the use of metal cramps and nails for reinforcing, and unnecessary concealment of nonfigural Byzantine work — could hardly escape Whittemore's notice. Fossati's workmen had filled gaps haphazardly and covered whole cubes with plaster: a cross was clumsily smeared with plaster, three fingers were obscured by lime, a foot was partially destroyed by unskillful restoration. Critical as he was of such blemishes, Whittemore conceded that Fossati's artisans had simply been ordered to cover the mosaics without delay, and "it would have been wasted effort for them to cleanse the surface before smearing over it their screen of pigment." His own experienced craftsmen, on the other hand, were able to carry out their "unhurried work" over a period of years.

Remarkably little of the original figural mosaic work had actually been lost during Fossati's hasty restoration, and although much had clearly been lost since Fossati's time — perhaps during the earthquake of 1894 — sur-

prisingly little harm had been done to the original decor. Within the limits of his own work on the surviving figural mosaics, Whittemore found no evidence of intentional destruction or willful mutilation of figures. Thus the Byzantine Institute of America was able to reveal works of the mosaicist's art much as they had looked a thousand years earlier.

The Americans' work covered, successively, the vaults and the walls of the narthex, the southwest vestibule, the south gallery, the apse, and the north tympanum. A steel scaffold, some forty feet high, was built in Istanbul for this purpose. Lighted and heated with electricity from the mosque, it had two sliding platforms enclosed in canvas from which the team worked. Whittemore was especially interested in the mosaic crosses thus uncovered in the lunettes of the narthex. At first sight similar, each proved in fact different from the other in the color of its jewels and its outline, and in the technique employed by its workmen. Whittemore observed that the early mosaicists worked "in accordance with their personal propensities," some handling the cubes with greater care and economy than others. He dates the crosses, together with certain other geometrical forms, to the original sixth-century church, claiming that they "offer a clue to the character which Justinian gave to the entire first interior decoration of the building, to reconcile the Monophysites to the official Church and thus strengthen his own position in the state."

In these works of art Whittemore emphasizes the contrast between the crosses of the sixth century and the great lunette of the ninth, located over the central imperial door, which portrays the figure of Christ and

ΙΩΆΝΝΗϹ Ο ΧΡΥϹΟϹΤΟΜΟϹ

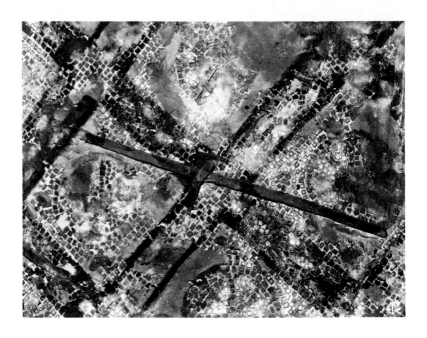

that of Emperor Leo VI prostrated before him. Here "the successful reaction against iconoclasm is marked by a renewal of classical influences; and the great mosaic is classical. . . . On the other hand the crosses reflect, in their immediate appeal to our emotional life, an approach to action that is more characteristic of Asia than of the mystical transfigurations of matter which have found favor in Europe." This central mosaic is, in Whittemore's view, one of the first works of art to appear in Hagia Sophia after the return of the icons. He brackets it with the tenth-century offertory panel over the door of the vestibule, which he likewise uncovered, as "two masterpieces of the art of mosaics of the Classical Renaissance which began in Constantinople in the second half of the ninth century." Both are "the works of Metropolitan masters, compared with which the contemporary mosaics in Italy, for instance, are provincial and derived."

Whittemore's imagination is kindled especially by the panel in the vestibule, the first object of beauty to be seen by the visitor entering the building. This he describes in lyrical terms:

> Viewed from below, the picture manifests itself to the beholder like a golden firmament. Beneath the Mother's clear, calm gaze the radiant image of the Child shines ethereal in the brightness of the throne and the footstool of jewelled silver. On either hand the tranquil Priest-Emperors crowned with gems, vested in irridescent robes and shod with light, offer their votive gifts with praise and supplication. The inscriptions are resplendent in glowing letters, tremulous as lines of lamps.

Light, as he sees it, is the essence of this mosaic; not simply light shed upon it from the south door, but light emanating from the mosaic itself, so that the throne on which the Virgin sits seems illuminated from within. Flanking the Virgin and Child is the ethereal figure of Constantine himself, presenting a scale model of his city. As Whittemore sees it, his wraithlike appearance contrasts sharply with the more materialized figure of Justinian, who presents a model of his church. Both have "careworn brows and furrowed cheeks," but both have been transformed into "celestial inhabitants . . . on the bourne between the spiritual and the actual worlds in the refulgent light of the impalpable universe."

Analyzing the mosaicist's technique, as shown in these two panels, Whittemore remarks on the gradual inward inclination of their surfaces from top to bottom — and concludes that the artist's intention was to deflect the light to the observer at the required angle. He also catalogued some fifty different tints used in the tesserae of the mosaics. Apart from gold and silver, they include: marble tones of yellow ocher, cadmium orange, and rose madder; as well as glass shades of chrome yellow, raw and burnt umber, hematite, indigo, purple, Van Dyke brown, viridian, ultramarine, and cobalt blue. Whittemore insists severely: "Use of mother-of-pearl is a provincial vulgarity and does not appear anywhere in the mosaics of Hagia Sophia."

One of the mosaics that Whittemore had sought but failed to find was a tenth-century portrait of the short-lived Emperor Alexander. A sketch by Fossati indicated that the mosaic had survived at least until 1849, and Whittemore assumed that it had been destroyed in the earthquake of 1894. Eight years after his death in

In the process of restoring Hagia Sophia's mosaics, Whittemore and his assistants discovered evidence of Fossati's haphazard and hasty methods a century earlier — such as his use of metal cramps to reinforce nonfigural mosaics (left). Among the drawings Fossati had made of the mosaics prior to covering them again was one of the tenth-century emperor Alexander. The panel was assumed lost or destroyed until 1958, when it was discovered in an inconspicuous spot in the north gallery, twenty feet above the pavement (right).

1950 at the age of 79, the mosaic was found, largely through the researches of Robert Van Nice, high above the floor on the opposite side of the nave from the other imperial portraits. Unlike the rest, it had been covered not with ordinary plaster but with a painted pattern in imitation of the surrounding mosaic decoration, and had thus escaped notice. It was duly cleaned and restored by Whittemore's successor at the Byzantine Institute, Dr. Paul A. Underwood. Whittemore's report on the mosaics in the apse, restored from a scaffold nearly 120 feet high, remained unfinished at the time of his death and was completed and published by Cyril Mango and Ernest J. W. Hawkins in 1964.

Three years later Pope Paul VI paid an official visit to the museum of Hagia Sophia. At one moment in the course of his tour of the restored apse an incident occurred that was to cause a small furor. Standing beneath the dome and looking eastward to the mosaic of the Virgin and Child, the pontiff turned to his hosts and said: "May I say a short prayer?" Then, without waiting for a reply, he knelt and murmured a Hail Mary. The incident was brief, but widely reported in the press, and a day later three leaders of the National Union of Students entered the museum and publicly performed a Moslem ritual prayer before the *mihrab*. Afterward they sent a picture of Mohammed the Conqueror to the Vatican, with the words of the Islamic prophecy inscribed beneath it: "Constantinople will one day be conquered." Momentarily, the great building had once more become a scene of religious controversy.

Hagia Sophia stands today as a great museum, restored and secure in the incomparable symmetry and scale of its architecture. Throughout the year it draws a steady flow of visitors of all faiths and from all parts of the world — a wider and more various world than the Byzantine Empire in its heyday ever conceived. They come to Hagia Sophia not as worshipers but as secular pilgrims, imbued with reverence for the foremost shrine of a great epoch of religion and civilization. The broad space of the nave, beneath the seemingly infinite space of the dome, recalls a huge piazza. Here modern visitors, dwarfed by the immensity of this area, stand and walk in wonder, gazing upward and around them, gathering in groups to hear the words of their guides as they echo throughout the vaults.

The building they see and admire, although bereft of many of its treasures and changed in much of its decorative detail, remains in essence the great church that Justinian's architects constructed fourteen hundred years ago. Visitors still marvel at the two-storied arcades that flank the nave; at the color and variety of the columns that support them, the very same that were brought to Justinian from all parts of his far-flung empire; at the lacework marble capitals that crown them; and at the moldings of the arches and architraves above. Looking eastward, they wonder at the majestic curve of the apse; looking westward, at the towering imperial portals with their lintels of bronze. Here and there gleam the mosaics that Whittemore described in phrases hardly less lofty than those of the sixth-century poet Paul the Silentiary. Hagia Sophia, enveloping all, is a masterpiece of space, light, proportion, and volume.

Through a collaboration between East and West, Hagia Sophia has been brought to life once more. If it

133

No subject was too minute or too grand for the artists who embellished Hagia Sophia. Stylized dolphins and marine animals (left) form a part of a recently cleaned inlaid-marble panel in the western wall of the nave. The archangel Gabriel (right), from the bema arch of the apse, is one of the crowning achievements of Byzantine art — and can also be regarded as a fitting symbol of the harmonious coexistence of Islamic and Christian traditions. To Christians, Gabriel is the angel of the Annunciation; to Moslems, he is the angel of truth who revealed the Koran to the Prophet.

is to remain a living building, the partnership between the government of the Turkish Republic and the Byzantine Institute of America at Dumbarton Oaks in Washington, D.C., must remain as close as ever. One result of that collaboration is the detailed architectural survey, conducted by William Emerson and Robert Van Nice, that was initiated by the institute before World War II and has been expanded since. Covering the whole of the vast and complex structure, it has enabled modern scholars to analyze the exact structural problems that faced Justinian's architects, outline their methods of tackling them, and identify the nature and extent of each subsequent reconstruction.

Within the building itself much still remains to be done, quite apart from the major task of removing Fossati's discolored and time-worn plasterwork. The glitter and gold of Hagia Sophia's surviving mosaics dazzle the beholder once again, but the cleaning and restoration of other parts of the building fall far short of perfection. This applies particularly to the panels, revetments, and columns brought from all parts of the Byzantine Empire — and so lyrically described by the Silentiary. "The marble pastures gathered on the lofty walls" no longer gleam as they once did in their infinite variety of color and pattern. Where today is that marble "not from some upland glen but from the level plains, in parts fresh green as the sea or emerald stone, or again like blue cornflowers in grass . . ."? What has become of Procopius's "meadow with its flowers in full bloom"?

All this still survives, of course. But today it is barely visible. The marbles of Hagia Sophia have lost their light and polish; the accumulated dust and grime of centuries dulls them. They no longer live as nature designed them. Man has allowed them to go dead, and only in one place can they be seen as the poets once described them. On the western wall of the nave, above and around the door, the craftsmen of the Byzantine Institute have cleaned and repaired the revetments, as previously they cleaned and repaired the bronze doors of the narthex. Their main object in doing so was to reveal five pictorial panels worked in an inlaid marble design. One of them, in white stone and black marble, represents a domed, ribbed canopy with a cross in the center and two birds above. Two others, flanking a slab of verd antique, represent dolphins of green porphyry feeding on marine creatures of a white dolomite rock.

These panels are works of art worthy in themselves of reclamation. In the course of uncovering them, the veined marble slabs of the surrounding wall have been brought as vividly to life once more. In just such a manner could life be restored to all the marble surfaces of Hagia Sophia, revealing their original brilliance. The Byzantine Institute has in recent years turned its resources to other important tasks, notably the cleaning and restoration of the mosaics and marbles of the Kariye mosque. The simple expedient of cleaning the finer and more numerous marbles of the time of Justinian, in similar if not indeed wider international partnership, would fully illuminate Hagia Sophia once more, and so revive its former pristine magic.

Only then will the great church-mosque-museum of the Holy Wisdom become wholly worthy of Atatürk's intention and of W. B. Yeats's lines on the glory of Constantinople:

> Miracle, bird or golden handiwork
> More miracle than bird or handiwork.

HAGIA SOPHIA
IN LITERATURE

Procopius of Caesarea's reputation as a historian rests primarily on his History
of the Wars, *a massive chronicle of Justinian's campaigns against the Persians,
Vandals, and Goths in the sixth century* A.D. *A privileged member of the court
at Constantinople — he served as private secretary to the emperor's outstanding
general, Belisarius — Procopius was an eyewitness to the events he recorded.
His later work,* Buildings, *is a fulsome panegyric to Justinian's numerous architectural additions to his far-flung empire — including the rebuilt church of
Hagia Sophia. Procopius's account is the definitive description of Hagia Sophia
and has been the basis for all subsequent studies.*

Some men of the common herd, all the rubbish of the city, once rose up
against the Emperor Justinian in Byzantium, when they brought about the
rising called the Nika Insurrection. . . . And by way of shewing that it was
not against the Emperor alone that they had taken up arms, but no less
against God himself, unholy wretches that they were, they had the hardihood
to fire the Church of the Christians, which the people of Byzantium call
"Sophia," an epithet which they have most appropriately invented for God,
by which they call His temple; and God permitted them to accomplish this
impiety, forseeing into what an object of beauty this shrine was destined
to be transformed. So the whole church at that time lay a charred mass of
ruins. But the Emperor Justinian built not long afterwards a church so finely
shaped, that if anyone had enquired of the Christians before the burning
if it would be their wish that the church should be destroyed and one like
this should take its place, shewing them some sort of model of the building
we now see, it seems to me that they would have prayed that they might
see their church destroyed forthwith, in order that the building might be
converted into its present form. At any rate the Emperor, disregarding all
questions of expense, eagerly pressed on to begin the work of construction,
and began to gather all the artisans from the whole world. And Anthemius
of Tralles, the most learned man in the skilled craft which is known as the
art of building, not only of all his contemporaries, but also when compared
with those who had lived long before him, ministered to the Emperor's
enthusiasm, duly regulating the tasks of the various artisans, and preparing
in advance designs of the future construction; and associated with him was
another master-builder, Isidorus by name, a Milesian by birth, a man who
was intelligent and worthy to assist the Emperor Justinian. Indeed this
also was an indication of the honour in which God held the Emperor, that
He had already provided the men who would be most serviceable to him
in the tasks which were waiting to be carried out. . . .

    . . . Both its breadth and its length have been so carefully proportioned,
that it may not improperly be said to be exceedingly long and at the same
time unusually broad. And it exults in an indescribable beauty. For it
proudly reveals its mass and the harmony of its proportions, having neither
any excess nor deficiency, since it is both more pretentious than the buildings
to which we are accustomed, and considerably more noble than those which
are merely huge, and it abounds exceedingly in sunlight and in the reflection
of the sun's rays from the marble. Indeed one might say that its interior is not
illuminated from without by the sun, but that the radiance comes into being
within it, such an abundance of light bathes this shrine. And the face itself
of the church (which would be the part which faces the rising sun, that
portion of the building in which they perform the mysteries in worship

of God) was constructed in the following manner. A structure of masonry is built up from the ground, not made in a straight line, but gradually curving inward on its flanks and receding at the middle, so that it forms the shape of half a circle, which those who are skilled in such matters call a half-cylinder; and so it rises precipitously to a height. The upper part of this structure ends in the fourth part of a sphere, and above it another crescent-shaped structure rises, fitted to the adjoining parts of the building, marvellous in its grace, but by reason of the seeming insecurity of its composition altogether terrifying. For it seems somehow to float in the air on no firm basis, but to be poised aloft to the peril of those inside it. Yet actually it is braced with exceptional firmness and security. On either side of this are columns arranged on the pavement; these likewise do not stand in a straight line, but they retreat inward in the pattern of the semicircle as if they were yielding to one another in a choral dance, and above them hangs a structure of crescent shape. And on the side opposite the east is reared a wall containing the entrances, and on either side of this there stand in a semi-circle not only the columns themselves but also the structure above them, all this being very similar to the columns and structure I have just described. And in the centre of the church stand four man-made eminences, which they call piers, two on the north side and two on the south, opposite and equal to each other, each pair having between them just four columns. The piers are composed of huge stones joined together, carefully selected and skilfully fitted to one another by the masons, and rising to a great height. One might suppose that they were sheer mountain-peaks. From these spring four arches which rise over the four sides of a square, and their ends come together in pairs and are made fast to each other on top of these piers, while the other portions rise and soar to an infinite height. And while two of the arches rise over empty air, those namely on the east and the west sides, the other two have under them certain structural elements, including a number of rather small columns. Upon the crowns of the arches rests a circular structure, cylindrical in shape; it is through this that the light of day always first smiles. . . . And upon this circle rests the huge spherical dome which makes the structure exceptionally beautiful. Yet it seems not to rest upon solid masonry, but to cover the space with its golden dome suspended from Heaven. All these details, fitted together with incredible skill in mid-air and floating off from each other and resting only on the parts next to them, produce a single and most extraordinary harmony in the work, and yet do not permit the spectator to linger much over the study of any one of them, but each detail attracts the eye and draws it on irresistibly to itself. So the vision constantly shifts suddenly, for the beholder is utterly unable to select which particular detail he should admire more than all the others. But even so, though they turn their attention to every side and look with contracted brows upon every detail, observers are still unable to understand the skilful craftsmanship. . . .

The whole ceiling is overlaid with pure gold, which adds glory to the beauty, yet the light reflected from the stones prevails, shining out in rivalry with the gold. And there are two stoa-like colonnades, one on each side, not separated in any way from the structure of the church itself, but actually making the effect of its width greater, and reaching along its whole length, to the very end, while in height they are less than the interior of the building. And they too have vaulted ceilings and decorations of gold. . . . But who

The eight lithographs depicting life in Constantinople that illustrate Hagia Sophia in Literature *(pages 138–60) are from* The Beauties of the Bosphorus, *a lively nineteenth-century travel narrative by an enterprising Englishwoman, Julia Pardoe.*

could fittingly describe the galleries . . . or enumerate the many colonnades and the colonnaded aisles by means of which the church is surrounded? Or who could recount the beauty of the columns and the stones with which the church is adorned? One might imagine that he had come upon a meadow with its flowers in full bloom. For he would surely marvel at the purple of some, the green tint of others, and at those on which the crimson glows and those from which the white flashes, and again at those which Nature, like some painter, varies with the most contrasting colours. And whenever anyone enters this church to pray, he understands at once that it is not by any human power or skill, but by the influence of God, that this work has been so finely turned. And so his mind is lifted up toward God and exalted, feeling that He cannot be far away, but must especially love to dwell in this place which He has chosen. And this does not happen only to one who sees the church for the first time, but the same experience comes to him on each successive occasion, as though the sight were new each time. Of this spectacle no one has ever had a surfeit, but when present in the church men rejoice in what they see, and when they leave it they take proud delight in conversing about it.

PROCOPIUS
Buildings, c. A.D. 560

Twelve centuries after Procopius's death, Edward Gibbon included a lengthy description of Justinian's magnificent church in his classic tome, The Decline and Fall of the Roman Empire. *As the following excerpt reveals, even the objective English historian was awed by Hagia Sophia.*

The new Cathedral of St. Sophia was consecrated by the patriarch, five years, eleven months, and ten days from the first foundation; and in the midst of the solemn festival Justinian exclaimed with devout vanity, "Glory be to God, who hath thought me worthy to accomplish so great a work; I have vanquished thee, O Solomon!" But the pride of the Roman Solomon, before twenty years had elapsed, was humbled by an earthquake, which overthrew the eastern part of the dome. Its splendor was again restored by the perseverance of the same prince; and in the thirty-sixth year of his reign, Justinian celebrated the second dedication of a temple, which remains, after twelve centuries, a stately monument of his fame. The architecture of St. Sophia, which is now converted into the principal mosque, has been imitated by the Turkish sultans, and that venerable pile continues to excite the fond admiration of the Greeks, and the more rational curiosity of European travellers. The eye of the spectator is disappointed by an irregular prospect of half-domes and shelving roofs: the western front, the principal approach, is destitute of simplicity and magnificence; and the scale of dimensions has been much surpassed by several of the Latin cathedrals. But the architect who first erected an *aerial* cupola, is entitled to the praise of bold design and skilful execution. . . . A Greek cross, inscribed in a quadrangle, represents the form of the edifice; the exact breadth is two hundred and forty-three feet, and two hundred and sixty-nine may be assigned for the extreme length from the sanctuary in the east, to the nine western doors which open into the vestibule, and from thence into the *narthex* or exterior portico. That portico was the humble station of the penitents. The nave or body of

the church was filled by the congregation of the faithful; but the two sexes were prudently distinguished, and the upper and lower galleries were allotted for the more private devotion of the women. Beyond the northern and southern piles, a balustrade, terminated on either side by the thrones of the emperor and the patriarch, divided the nave from the choir; and the space, as far as the steps of the altar, was occupied by the clergy and singers. The altar itself, a name which insensibly became familiar to Christian ears, was placed in the eastern recess, artificially built in the form of a demi-cylinder; and this sanctuary communicated by several doors with the sacristy, the vestry, the baptistery, and the contiguous buildings, subservient either to the pomp of worship, or the private use of ecclesiastical ministers. The memory of the past calamities inspired Justinian with a wise resolution, that no wood, except for the doors, should be admitted into the new edifice; and the choice of the materials was applied to the strength, the lightness, or the splendor of the respective parts. The solid piles which contained the cupola were composed of huge blocks of freestone, hewn into squares and triangles, fortified by circles of iron, and firmly cemented by the infusion of lead and quicklime. . . .

A poet [Paul the Silentiary], who beheld the primitive lustre of St. Sophia, enumerates the colors, the shades, and the spots of ten or twelve marbles, jaspers, and porphyries, which nature had profusely diversified, and which were blended and contrasted as it were by a skilful painter. The triumph of Christ was adorned with the last spoils of Paganism, but the greater part of these costly stones was extracted from the quarries of Asia Minor, the isles and continent of Greece, Egypt, Africa, and Gaul. Eight columns of porphyry, which Aurelian had placed in the temple of the sun, were offered by the piety of a Roman matron; eight others of green marble were presented by the ambitious zeal of the magistrates of Ephesus: both are admirable by their size and beauty, but every order of architecture disclaims their fantastic capitals. A variety of ornaments and figures was curiously expressed in mosaic; and the images of Christ, of the Virgin, of saints, and of angels, which have been defaced by Turkish fanaticism, were dangerously exposed to the superstition of the Greeks. According to the sanctity of each object, the precious metals were distributed in thin leaves or in solid masses. The balustrade of the choir, the capitals of the pillars, the ornaments of the doors and galleries, were of gilt bronze; the spectator was dazzled by the glittering aspect of the cupola; the sanctuary contained forty thousand pound weight of silver; and the holy vases and vestments of the altar were of the purest gold, enriched with inestimable gems. Before the structure of the church had risen two cubits above the ground, forty-five thousand two hundred pounds were already consumed; and the whole expense amounted to three hundred and twenty thousand. Each reader, according to the measure of his belief, may estimate their value either in gold or silver; but the sum of one million sterling is the result of the lowest computation. A magnificent temple is a laudable monument of national taste and religion; and the enthusiast who entered the dome of St. Sophia might be tempted to suppose that it was the residence, or even the workmanship, of the Deity. Yet how dull is the artifice, how insignificant is the labor, if it be compared, with the formation of the vilest insect that crawls upon the surface of the temple.

EDWARD GIBBON

The Decline and Fall of the Roman Empire, 1781

*An obscure French knight from Picardy, Robert of Clari entered Constantinople
in 1204 with the victorious armies of the Fourth Crusade. His account of the
Latin conquest of Christendom's richest and most civilized city is both reliable
and colorful. With a simple tourist's ingenuousness, Robert marveled at Hagia
Sophia and the religious legends reported by Greek interpreters.*

The pilgrims regarded the great size of the city, and the palaces and fine
abbeys and churches and the great wonders which were in the city, and
they marveled at it greatly. And they marveled greatly at the church of
Saint Sophia and at the riches which were in it.

Now I will tell you about the church of Saint Sophia, how it was made. . . .
The church of Saint Sophia was entirely round, and within the church
there were domes, round all about, which were borne by great and very
rich columns, and there was no column which was not of jasper or porphyry
or some other precious stone, nor was there one of these columns that did
not work cures. There was one that cured sickness of the reins when it was
rubbed against, and another that cured sickness of the side, and others that
cured other ills. And there was no door in this church and no hinges or bands
or other parts such as are usually made of iron that were not all of silver. The
master altar of the church was so rich that it was beyond price, for the
table of the altar was made of gold and precious stones broken up and
crushed all together, which a rich emperor had had made. This table was
fully fourteen feet long. Around the altar were columns of silver supporting
a canopy over the altar which was made just like a church spire, and it was
all of solid silver and was so rich that no one could tell the money it was
worth. The place where they read the gospel was so fair and noble that
we could not describe to you how it was made. Then down through the
church there hung fully a hundred chandeliers, and there was not one that
did not hang by a great silver chain as thick as a man's arm. And there
were in each chandelier full five and twenty lamps or more. . . . On the ring
of the great door of the church, which was all of silver, there hung a tube,
of what material no one knew; it was the size of a pipe such as shepherds
play on. This tube had such virtue as I shall tell you. When an infirm man
who had some sickness in his body like the bloat, so that he was bloated
in his belly, put it in his mouth, however little he put it in, when this tube
took hold it sucked out all the sickness and it made the poison run out of
his mouth and it held him so fast that it made his eyes roll and turn in
his head, and he could not get away until the tube had sucked all of this
sickness out of him. And the sicker a man was the longer it held him, and
if a man who was not sick put it in his mouth, it would not hold him at all,
much or little.

Then in front of this church of Saint Sophia there was a great column
which was fully three times the reach of a man's arms in thickness and was
fully fifty *toises* [approximately 315 feet] in height. It was made of marble
and of copper over the marble and was bound about with strong bands of
iron. And on top of this column there lay a flat slab of stone which was fully
fifteen feet in length and as much in width. On this stone there was an
emperor [Justinian] made of copper on a great copper horse, and he was
holding out his hand toward heathendom. . . .

ROBERT OF CLARI
The Conquest of Constantinople, c. 1204

Born in Tangier in 1304, ibn-Battuta was the most indefatigable Arabian traveler of the Middle Ages. His ceaseless curiosity led him to traverse large regions of Europe, Africa, and Asia Minor. In Constantinople — which had been reconquered by the Byzantines in 1261 — this devout Moslem obtained an audience with the reigning Greek emperor, Andronicus III, and was later accompanied on a tour of "Ayā Sūfiyā" by the emperor's father.

I can describe only its exterior; as for its interior I did not see it. It is called in their language *Ayā Sūfiyā,* and the story goes that it was an erection of Āsaf the son of Barakhyā, who was the son of the maternal aunt of Solomon (on whom be peace). It is one of the greatest churches of the Greeks; around it is a wall which encircles it so that it looks like a city [in itself]. Its gates are thirteen in number, and it has a sacred enclosure, which is about a mile long and closed by a great gate. No one is prevented from entering the enclosure, and in fact I went into it with the king's father . . . ; it is like an audience-hall, paved with marble and traversed by a water-channel which issues from the church. This [flows between] two walls about a cubit high, constructed in marble inlaid with pieces of different colours and cut with the most skilful art, and trees are planted in rows on both sides of the channel. From the gate of the church to the gate of this hall there is a lofty pergola made of wood, covered with grape-vines and at the foot with jasmine and scented herbs. Outside the gate of this hall is a large wooden pavilion containing platforms, on which the guardians of this gate sit, and to the right of the pavilions are benches and booths, mostly of wood, in which sit their qāḍīs [Moslem religious judges] and the recorders of their bureaux. In the middle of the booths is a wooden pavilion, to which one ascends by a flight of wooden steps; in this pavilion is a great chair swathed in woollen cloth on which their qāḍī sits. . . . To the left of the pavilion which is at the gate of this hall is the bazaar of the druggists. The canal that we have described divides into two branches. . . .

At the door of the church there are porticoes where the attendants sit who sweep its paths, light its lamps and close its doors. They allow no person to enter it until he prostrates himself to the huge cross at their place, which they claim to be a relic of the wood on which the double of Jesus (on whom be peace) was crucified. This is over the door of the church, set in a golden frame about ten cubits in height, across which they have placed a similar golden frame so that it forms a cross. This door is covered with plaques of silver and gold, and its two rings are of pure gold. I was told that the number of monks and priests in this church runs into thousands, and that some of them are descendants of the Apostles, also that inside it is another church exclusively for women, containing more than a thousand virgins consecrated to religious devotions, and a still greater number of aged and widowed women. It is the custom of the king, his officers of state, and the rest of the inhabitants to come to visit this church every morning, and the Pope comes to it once in the year. When he is at a distance of four nights' journey from the town the king goes out to meet him and dismounts before him; when he enters the city, the king walks on foot in front of him, and comes to salute him every morning and evening during the whole period of his stay in Constantinople until he departs.

IBN-BATTUTA
The Travels, 1325–54

When Pero Tafur, a Spanish nobleman from Cordova, arrived in Constantinople in 1437 he found the once-proud city poor, neglected, and governed by a corrupt administration. Within twenty years of his visit, the decaying Byzantine Empire would fall to the invading Ottoman Turks. Remarkably enough under the circumstances, Hagia Sophia still retained much of its former glory.

I went to the Despot, and asked him if he would be pleased to direct that I should be shown the church of St. Sophia and its relics, and he replied that he would do it with pleasure, and that he himself desired to go there to hear Mass, as did also the Empress and her brother, the real Emperor of Trebizond. We then went to the church to Mass, and afterwards they caused the church to be shown to me. It is very large and they say that in the days of the prosperity of Constantinople there were in it six thousand clergy. Inside, the circuit is for the most part badly kept, but the church itself is in such fine state that it seems to-day to have only just been finished. It is made in the Greek manner with many lofty chapels, roofed with lead, and inside there is a profusion of mosaic work to a spear's length from the ground. This mosaic work is so fine that not even a brush could attempt to better it. Below are very delicate stones, intermixed with marble, porphyry, and jasper, very richly worked. The floor is made of great stones, most delicately cut, which are very magnificent. In the centre of these chapels is the principal one which is very large; the height is such that it is difficult to believe that cement can hold it together. In this chapel there is similar mosaic work, with a figure of God the Father in the centre. From below it looks the size of an ordinary man, but they say that the foot is as long as a spear, and from eye to eye the distance is many spans in length. Here is the great altar, and here one can see all the grace and richness appertaining to geometry. Beneath this chapel there is a great cistern which, they say, could contain a ship of 3000 *botas* in full sail, the breadth, height and depth of water being all sufficient. . . .

The Despot and the others directed the clergy to bring out the holy relics. The Despot keeps one key, and the Patriarch of Constantinople, who was there, the other. The third is kept by the Prior of the church. The clergy, in their vestments, brought out the relics in procession, which were: Firstly the lance which pierced Our Lord's side, a marvellous relic; the coat without a seam, which must at one time have been violet, but which had now grown grey with age; one of the nails; and some thorns from Our Lord's crown, with many others, such as the wood of the Cross, and the pillar at which Our Lord was scourged. There were also several things of Our Blessed Lady the Virgin, and the gridiron on which St. Lawrence was roasted, and many other relics which St. Helena took when she was at Jerusalem and carried here, which are much reverenced and closely guarded. God grant that in the overthrow of the Greeks they have not fallen into the hands of the enemies of the Faith, for they will have been ill-treated and handled with little reverence. As we came out we saw at the door of the church a great column of stone, higher than the great chapel itself, and on the top is a great horse of gilded brass, upon which is a knight with one arm raised, pointing with the finger towards Turkey, and in the other he holds an orb, as a sign that all the world is in his hand. . . .

PERO TAFUR
Travels and Adventures, c. 1455

Evliya Chelebi was a descendant of a standard-bearer at the Turkish conquest of Constantinople and the son of the city's chief goldsmith. In his youth he was a superlative student of the Koran and served briefly as a page to Sultan Murad IV. In 1631, at the age of twenty-one, Evliya had a vision in which the Prophet urged him to travel throughout the world, visiting the tombs of the saints. He began his calling in his native city, with a study of the principal mosques. From his description, one would scarcely guess that for most of its thousand years Hagia Sophia had been consecrated to Christian worship and had been a Moslem mosque for less than two centuries.

The first, and most ancient of these places of worship dedicated to the almighty and everlasting God, is that of Ayá Sófiya. . . . It was finished by Ignatius, a perfect architect, well skilled in geometry, under the direction of the Prophet Khizr; and forty thousand workmen, seven thousand porters, and three thousand builders, were employed in raising its domes and arches on three thousand pillars. Every part of the world was ransacked to find the richest marbles, and the hardest stones for its walls and columns. Stones of various hues, fit for the throne of Belkis, were brought from Ephesus and Aïdinjik; marbles of divers colours were removed from Karamán, Syria, and the island of Cyprus. Some thousands of incomparable columns, wasp and olive-coloured, were imported from the splendid monuments of the skill of Solomon, standing in the neighbourhood of Athens. After working at the building for forty years, Khizr and Ignatius disappeared one night when they had finished half the dome. Seven years afterwards they appeared again and completed it. On its summit they placed a cross of gold an hundred Alexandrian quintals in weight, visible at Brúsah, Mount Olympus, 'Alemdághí, and Istránjeh dághí. On the birth-night of the Prophet there was a dreadful earthquake, by which this and many other wonderful domes were thrown down; but it was afterwards restored by the aid of Khizr, and by the advice of the Prophet, to whom the three hundred patriarchs and monks, presiding over the church, were sent by him. As a memorial of the restoration of the dome by the aid of the Prophet and Khizr, Mohammed the Conqueror suspended in the middle of it, by a golden chain, a Golden Globe, which can hold fifty kílahs of grain, Roman measure; it is within reach of a man's hand, and beneath it Khizr performed his service to God. Among the pious, many persons have chosen the same place for offering up their orisons [prayers]; and several who have persevered in saying the morning prayer there for forty days, have obtained the blessings, temporal and spiritual, for which they prayed: it is, therefore, much frequented by the pious and necesitous for that purpose.

This mosque is situated on elevated ground at the eastern end of the city, a thousand paces distant from the Stable-gate near the sea, and a thousand from Seraglio Point. The great cupola which rears its head into the skies is joined by a half-cupola, beneath which is the mihráb [sacred recess], and to the right of it a marble pulpit [*minbar*]. There are altogether on the whole building no less then 360 gilt cupolas, the largest of which is the great one in the middle; they are ornamented with broad, circular, and crystal glasses, the number of which in the whole mosque amounts to 1,070. The abovementioned cupolas are adorned within by wonderful paintings, representing cherubims and men, the work of Monástir, a painter, skilful as Arzheng. These figures seem even now, to a silent and reflecting observer,

to be possessed of life and thought. Besides them, there are, at the four angles supporting the great cupola, four angels, no doubt the four archangels, Gabriel, Michael, Isráfíl, and 'Azráyíl, standing with their wings extended, each 56 cubits high. Before the birth of the Prophet, these four angels used to speak, and give notice of all dangers which threatened the empire and the city of Islámból [Istanbul], but since his Highness appeared, all talismans have ceased to act. This cupola is supported by four arches that excel the arch of the palace of Chosroes, the arch of Khavernak; that of Kaïdafà; that of Káf, and that of Sheddád. The large columns, of the richest colours and most precious marble, are forty Mecca-cubits high; those of the second story are not less beautiful, but are only thirty cubits high. There are two galleries running round three sides of this mosque, and forming upper mosques for the worshippers; there is an ascent to them on both sides, which may be ascended on horseback; it is a royal road paved with white marble. The mosque has altogether 361 doors, of which 101 are large gates, through which large crowds can enter. They are all so bewitched by talismans, that if you count them ever so many times, there always appears to be one more than there was before. They are each twenty cubits high, and are adorned with goldsmith's work and enamel. The middle gate towards the Kiblah, which is the highest of all, is fifty cubits high. It is made of planks from the ark which Noah constructed with his own hand. . . .

Above it, in a niche, supported on small columns, stands a picture of Jerusalem, in marble; within it there are jewels of inestimable value, but it is also talismanic, and cannot be touched by any body. In this place there stood likewise upon a green column an image of the Virgin Mary, holding in her hand a carbuncle as big as a pigeon's egg, by the blaze of which the mosque was lighted every night. . . .

If any man have a bad memory which he wishes to improve, he should place himself beneath the Golden Ball suspended in the middle of the cupola, and say the morning prayer seven times; three times repeat the words O God who openest all difficult things and knowest all secret and hidden things, and each time eat seven black grapes, and then whatever he hears will remain fixed in his memory as if engraven on stone. A most noted example of this was Hamdí Chelebí. . . . No doctors could do him any good, so that at last he was completely a prey to forgetfulness, till he went . . . to Ayá Sófiyah, where, after saying the requisite prayers, and eating the grapes as prescribed above, beneath the Golden Ball, he was so completely cured of his stupidity, that he began immediately to compose his poem of Yusuf and Zuleïkhá, which he finished in seven months; after which he wrote his Treatise on Physiognomy, which is known all over the world. . . .

On the east side of the upper gallery there are five or six smooth flat slabs of various coloured stones, which reflect the rays of the rising sun with so bright a light that the eye of man cannot look stedfastly on them. . . . The whole of this mosque is also covered with lead, which has remained uninjured for so many thousand years from its being mixed up with some thousand quintals of gold. All architects are lost in astonishment at the solidity of the foundations of this vast building, and no tongue or pen is capable of adequately describing it. We have seen the mosques of all the world; but never one like this.

EVLIYA CHELEBI
Narrative of Travels, c. 1635

Joseph Tournefort, chief botanist to Louis XIV and a member of the Royal Academy of Sciences, embarked on a scientific expedition to the Levant in 1700. His purpose was to study geography and natural history, but in Constantinople he could not resist visiting the principal sights — and he reluctantly concluded that Hagia Sophia compared favorably with the cathedrals of France.

The first Walk a Stranger usually takes in *Constantinople,* is to the Royal Mosques, of which there are seven so call'd. These Edifices, which are very handsom in their kind, are compleatly finish'd, and kept in perfect good condition; whereas in *France* we have scarce such a thing as a finish'd Church: if the Nave is admired for its Largeness and Beauty of its Arch-work, the Choir is imperfect; if these two parts are compleat, the Frontispiece is not begun. Most of our Churches, especially in *Paris,* are hedg'd in with profane Buildings, and Tradesmens Shops, to make advantage of every the least Spot of Ground; the Church is often so chok'd up with Houses, there's no Avenue, no Vacancy left; whereas the Mosques of *Constantinople* stand single, within a spacious Inclosure, planted with fine Trees, adorn'd with delicate Fountains: they suffer not a Dog to enter; no one presumes to hold discourse there, or do the least irreverent Action: they are well endow'd, and far exceed ours in Riches: tho' their Architecture is inferior to ours, yet they fail not to make an impression on the Beholder by their Largeness and Solidity. . . .

St. Sophia is the most perfect of all these Mosques: its Situation is advantageous, for it stands in one of the best and finest Parts of *Constantinople,* at top of the ancient *Byzantium,* and of an Eminence that descends gradually down to the Sea by the Point of the Seraglio. This Church, which is certainly the finest Structure in the World next to St. *Peter's* at *Rome,* looks to be very unwieldy without: the Plan is almost square, and the Dome, which is the only thing worth remarking, rests outwardly on four prodigious large Towers, which have been added of late Years to support this vast Building, and make it immoveable, in a Country where whole Cities are often overthrown by Earthquakes. . . .

From the East part of [the] Dome you pass straight on to the Demi-dome, which terminates the Edifice. This Dome, or Shell, was the Sanctuary of the Christians, and the great Altar was placed there. *Mahomet* II. having conquer'd this City, went and sat here with his Legs cross'd under him after the manner of the *Turks*; after saying his Prayers, he caus'd himself to be shaved, and then fasten'd to one of the Pillars, where was the Patriarch's Throne, a fine piece of embroider'd Stuff, with *Arabick* Characters on it, which had serv'd as a Skreen in the Mosque of *Meca.* Such was the Consecration of *St. Sophia!* . . .

. . . They assured me there were no fewer than 107 Columns of different Marble, of Porphyry, or *Egyptian* Granate: we had not time to count 'em ourselves. The whole Dome is lined or pav'd with Varieties of Marble: the Incrustations of the Gallery are Mosaick, mostly done with Cubes or Dice of Glass, which are loosen'd every Day from their Cement, but their Colour is unalterable. These glass Dice are real Doublets, for the variegated Leaf is cover'd with a piece of Glass very thin, and glued on, so as nothing but hot boiling Water can make it scale off: if ever Mosaicks should come again in fashion among us, we could easily do the like.

JOSEPH TOURNEFORT
A Voyage into the Levant, 1700

LADIES
IN THE MOSQUE

During the early years of the nineteenth century, the mosques of Constantinople were officially closed to Western, non-Moslem visitors, and only by an extra-ordinary effort could one gain admittance. Despite the danger of detection, Julia Pardoe — an energetic Englishwoman and the author of numerous travel books — was determined to see the interior of Hagia Sophia.

During a visit that I made to a Turkish family, with whom I had become acquainted, the conversation turned on the difficulty of obtaining a Firman [license] to see the mosques; when it was stated that Baron Rothschild was the only private individual to whom the favour had ever been accorded . . . and that travellers were thus dependent on the uncertain chance of encountering, during their residence in Turkey, some distinguished person to whom the marble doors were permitted to fall back.

In vain I questioned and cross-questioned; I failed to obtain a ray of hope. . . .

Hours passed away, and other subjects had succeeded to this most interesting one, when, as the evening closed in, I remarked that —— Bey, the eldest son of the house, was carrying on a very energetic *sotto voce* conversation with his venerable father; and I was not a little astonished when he ultimately informed me, in his imperfect French, that there was one method of visiting the mosques, if I had the nerve to attempt it, which would probably prove successful; and that, in the event of my resolving to run the risk, he was himself so convinced of its practicability that he would accompany me, with the consent of his father, attended by the old Kiära, or House-steward; upon the understanding (and on this the grey-bearded Effendi had resolutely insisted) that in the event of detection it was to be *sauve qui peut* [each man for himself]; an arrangement that would enable his son at once to elude pursuit, if he exercised the least ingenuity or caution.

What European traveller, possessed of the least spirit of adventure, would refuse to encounter danger in order to stand beneath the dome of St. Sophia? And, above all, what wandering Giaour [unbeliever] could resist the temptation of entering a mosque during High Prayer? . . .

I at once understood that the attempt must be made in a Turkish dress; but this fact was of trifling importance, as no costume in the world lends itself more readily or more conveniently to the purposes of disguise. After having deliberately weighed the chances for and against detection, I resolved to run the risk; and accordingly I stained my eyebrows with some of the dye common in the harem; concealed my female attire beneath a magnificent pelisse, lined with sables, which fastened from my chin to my feet; pulled a *fèz* low upon my brow; and, preceded by a servant with a lantern, attended by the Bey, and followed by the Kiära and a pipe-bearer, at half past ten o'clock I sallied forth on my adventurous errand. . . .

"If we escape from St. Sophia unsuspected," said my chivalrous friend, "we will then make another bold attempt; we will visit the mosque of Sultan Achmet; and as this is a high festival, if you risk the adventure, you will have done what no Infidel has ever yet dared to do; but I forewarn you that, should you be discovered, and fail to make your escape on the instant, you will be torn to pieces."

This assertion somewhat staggered me, and for an instant my woman-spirit quailed; I contented myself, however, with briefly replying: "When we leave St. Sophia, we will talk of this," and continued to walk beside him in silence. At length we entered the spacious court of the mosque, and as the servants stooped to withdraw my shoes, the Bey murmured in my ear: "Be firm, or you are lost!" — and making a strong effort to subdue the feeling of mingled awe and fear, which was rapidly stealing over me, I pulled the *fèz* deeper upon my eye-brows, and obeyed.

On passing the threshold, I found myself in a covered peristyle, whose gigantic columns of granite are partially sunk in the wall of which they form a part; the floor was covered with fine matting, and the coloured lamps, which were suspended in festoons from the lofty ceiling, shed a broad light on all the surrounding objects. In most of the recesses formed by the pillars, beggars were crouched down, holding in front of them their little metal basins, to receive the *paras* of the charitable; while servants lounged to and fro, or squatted in groups upon the matting, awaiting the egress of their employers. As I looked around me, our own attendant moved forward, and raising the curtain which veiled a double door of bronze, situated at mid-length of the peristyle, I involuntarily shrank back before the blaze of light that burst upon me.

Far as the eye could reach upwards, circles of coloured fire, appearing as if suspended in mid-air, designed the form of the stupendous dome; while beneath, devices of every shape and colour were formed by myriads of lamps of various hues: the Imperial closet, situated opposite to the pulpit, was one blaze of refulgence, and its gilded lattices flashed back the brilliancy, till it looked like a gigantic meteor!

As I stood a few paces within the doorway, I could not distinguish the limits of the edifice — I looked forward, upward — to the right hand, and to the left — but I could only take in a given space, covered with human beings, kneeling in regular lines, and at a certain signal bowing their turbaned heads to the earth, as if one soul and one impulse animated the whole congregation; while the shrill chanting of the choir pealed through the vast pile, and died away in lengthened cadences among the tall dark pillars which support it.

And this was St. Sophia! To me it seemed like a creation of enchantment — the light — the ringing voices — the mysterious extent, which baffled the earnestness of my gaze — the ten thousand turbaned Moslems, all kneeling with their faces turned towards Mecca, and at intervals laying their foreheads to the earth — the bright and various colours of the dresses — and the rich and glowing tints of the carpets that veiled the marble floor — all conspired to form a scene of such unearthly magnificence, that I felt as though there could be no reality in what I looked on, but that, at some sudden signal, the towering columns would fail to support the vault of light above them, and all would become void.

I had forgotten every thing in the mere exercise of vision; — the danger of detection — the flight of time — almost my own identity — when my companion uttered the single word "*Gel* — Come" — and, passing forward to another door on the opposite side of the building, I instinctively followed him, and once more found myself in the court.

What a long breath I drew, as the cold air swept across my forehead! I felt like one who has suddenly stepped beyond the circle of an enchanter, and dissolved the spell of some mighty magic.

JULIA PARDOE
The City of the Sultan, 1837

As the wife of the British ambassador to the sultan's court in 1881, Lady Hariot Dufferin was a privileged Westerner and had no difficulty entering Hagia Sophia. Although accustomed to unusual experiences — she had accompanied her husband on prior diplomatic assignments to India, Canada, and Russia — the solemnity of the Moslem service made a lasting impression.

We reached St. Sophia at half-past eight, and, being a little early, the church was only half lighted. Our places were in a gallery, and we reached it by steep winding pathways (not stairs), a man walking before us holding a dim light. When we reached our seats we looked down upon the immense space — quantities of chandeliers far below us, and children rushing about, shrieking and thoroughly enjoying their enormous playground. St. Sophia having been built for a Christian church, the altar did not face quite the right way for the Mahomedans, and so everything in it is a little askew, which has a curious effect. . . .

It was lighted with oil-lamps, rows and rows of them; one row round the dome, which is very beautiful, and which in the day-time looks as if it was resting upon nothing.

Soon we heard the call to prayers, and the place filled rapidly. The men came in carrying their boots, and all placed themselves in lines, with spaces between each. I never saw anything more impressive than the service. There was the melancholy and barbarous wail of the priest reading the Koran, and every now and then more voices joining in, then a rustle, when the whole congregation bent forward, and then the sound as of a great wave, when they all fell down upon their knees, with their faces on the ground. The sight of all these human beings in the attitude of profoundest humility was most striking, and, although dead silence prevailed, one seemed to feel "Lord have mercy upon us, miserable sinners," in the air.

The same thing happened over and over again, but it always produced the same effect upon me. Self-abasement, adoration, devotion, all seemed thoroughly expressed by the service, and one scarcely knew which was most effective, the barbaric wail or the moments of silent meditation.

People differ about it as a sight; some say there is nothing to see, that it is all dull, etc. I think it one of the grandest things I ever saw, and, seated far above these people, I felt as if I was assisting at a dream, a sort of revelation, and not at a real church service. . . .

. . . [We] went to St. Sophia [again, a week later].

It is beautifully lighted, and looks much finer by day than at night, as one can see its enormous size, and admire the mosaic ceilings, and the beautiful marble columns, with their carved capitals.

We shuffled along in the slippers we were given at the door, and, in addition to the building, we saw an interesting service going on. A preacher was expounding the Koran, and round him sat the faithful with their hands reverently spread out, and giving him the warmest expressions of approval by constantly calling out, with great fervour, "Amen," or "God is great."

In another part of the church was a second preacher, and all about its vast proportions lay, sat, or knelt people sleeping, reading the Koran, listening, or praying. We thought they looked askance at us, and I am sure our presence is disagreeable to them.

LADY HARIOT DUFFERIN
My Russian and Turkish Journals, 1881

The lure of exotic Constantinople attracted many European literary figures during the nineteenth century. Théophile Gautier, a prominent French poet, novelist, and drama critic, was overwhelmed by Hagia Sophia.

To reach the entrance of the mosque, the visitor follows a narrow street, lined with sycamores, and with turbés [Moslem tombs] whose gilded and painted stone-work gleams vaguely through their gratings; and he arrives, after a few divergences, in front of a gate of bronze, one leaf of which still retains the imprint of the Greek cross. This is a side entrance, which gives access to a vestibule pierced with nine doors. At this point, the visitor exchanges his boots or shoes for slippers, which it is important to have brought by the dragoman; because to enter the mosque in boots would be as palpable an irreverence as to keep one's hat on in a Catholic church; and might, moreover, entail results by no means agreeable to the offender.

At the first step within, I was struck with amazement. I seemed to be at Venice, and entering from the Piazza, beneath the nave of Saint-Mark; only that the dimensions had enlarged immeasurably, and assumed colossal proportions. The columns rose gigantic, from the mat-covered pavement; the dome of the cupola hung overhead like the arch of the sky; the galleries, in which the four sacred streams pour forth their waters in mosaic, described immeasurable circuits; the tribunes seemed destined to contain whole nations! Saint-Mark, in fact, is but a miniature of Saint-Sophia; reduced, on the scale of an inch to a foot, from the basilica of Justinian. Nor is there anything surprising in this; for Venice, separated by only a narrow sea from Greece, lived always in familiarity with the Orient; and her architects would naturally seek to reproduce the type of that church, which was then considered the richest and the most beautiful of all Christendom. . . .

Although Islamism, in its hostility to the pictorial and plastic arts, has despoiled Saint-Sophia of the greater part of its noblest ornaments, it is still a magnificent edifice. The mosaics, upon a ground of gold, representing Scriptural subjects, like those of Saint Mark, have disappeared beneath a coating of lime. They have preserved the four gigantic cherubim of the galleries; the six wings of each shine through the scintillations of masses of gilded crystal; but the heads of these masses of gorgeous plumage are hidden behind enormous golden suns; the representation of the human face being the especial horror of the Moslemah. At the end of the sanctuary, beneath the oven-like arch which forms its termination, are vaguely traceable the outlines of a colossal figure, which the deposit of the lime has not altogether obliterated; this was the image of the patron of the church, — an embodiment of the Divine Wisdom in an individual form, the *Agia-Sophia*; and which, beneath this half-transparent veil, still presides over the ceremonies of a hostile faith.

The statues have been removed. The altar, made of an unknown metal, — the result, like the Corinthian brass, of a combination of gold, silver, bronze, iron, and, precious stones, in a state of fusion, — is replaced by a slab of red marble, indicating the direction of Mecca. Above, hangs an old and worn carpet, a mere dirty rag, which possesses, for the Turks, the unspeakable merit of being one of the four carpets on which Mahomet himself knelt to perform his devotions.

Immense green disks, given by different Sultans, are attached to the walls, and inscribed with verses from the Koran, or pious maxims, written in enormous golden letters. A scroll of porphyry bears the name of Allah, or Mahomet, and of the first four Kalifs: Abu-Bekir, Omar, Osman, and Ali. The pulpit (*nimbar*), where the *khatib* stands to read the Koran, is placed against one of the pillars, and is reached by a steep staircase, decorated with two balustrades of open carving, of a delicacy unsurpassed by that of the finest lace. The reader always ascends with the Book of the Law in one hand and a drawn sabre in the other, as in a conquered mosque.

Cords, from which are suspended tufts of silk, and ostrich eggs, hang from the dome to within ten or twelve feet of the floor, sustaining circles of iron wire decorated with lamps to form a chandelier. Desks in the form of an X, similar to those which we used to support portfolios of engravings, are dispersed about the mosque, to support manuscripts of the Koran. Many are ornamented with enamel, or delicate inlayings of brass, or mother-of-pearl.

Mats of rushes in the summer, and carpets in the winter, cover the pavement, formed of slabs of marble, the veins of which are skilfully arranged, to give the appearance of three streams, congealed, as they flow in wavy undulations through the edifice. The mats also present a singular peculiarity; they are placed obliquely, and contrary to the lines of architecture; like the planks of a floor, placed diagonally, instead of parallel, to the walls which enclose them. But this strange peculiarity is soon explained. Saint-Sophia was not originally designed for a mosque, and consequently does not stand in the proper direction, relatively to Mecca.

Many of the mosques much resemble, internally, Protestant churches, or rather "chapels." Art is not there allowed to display its elegancies. Pious inscriptions, a pulpit, reading desks, mats to cover the floors; and you have all the "ornament" that is permitted. The one idea of DEITY should fill His temple, and is sufficiently vast to do so unassisted. . . .

The chief cupola of Saint-Sophia, a little broken in its curve, is surrounded by several half-domes, like those of Saint-Mark. It is of immense height, and must have shone like a sun of gold and mosaic, before the Moslem coating of lime extinguished its splendors. But, such as it was, it produced upon me an impression even more startling than the dome of Saint Peter. The Byzantine architecture is certainly the style necessary for Catholicism. Even Gothic architecture, whatever its religious value, is not so perfectly adapted to this object. Despite its deteriorations of all sorts, Saint-Sophia still surpasses all Christian churches that I have seen; and I have seen many. Nothing can equal the majesty of its domes; the tribunes resting against its columns of jasper, of porphyry, and of verd-antique, with their strange Corinthian capitals; or the animals, the chimeras, and the crosses, enlaced among its sculptured foliage. . . .

During the progress of [his recent restorations], Signor Fossati had the curiosity to exhume many of the primitive mosaics, from the bed of lime in which they were buried; and, before covering them again, he caused them to be carefully copied; a proceeding, the fruits of which, it is to be hoped, may be one day given to the world.

These mosaics are those of the cupola and the demi-domes. The others, which decorate the lower walls, may be regarded as destroyed. The *mollahs* [Moslem religious teachers] remove, almost daily, with their knives, cubes of crystal, covered with gold leaf, and sell them to strangers. I myself possess some half-dozen of these, detached in my presence; for, although I am *not* one of these tourists who break off the noses of statues, as a souvenir of the monuments they have visited, I could not disappoint the hope of gratuity which inspired the worthy Moslem who offered me these memorials.

From the height of the tribunes (which are reached by gentle winding slopes, as in the Giralda or the Campanilla), an admirable view of the mosque is obtained. At this moment, some faithful believers, kneeling upon the matting, are devoutly performing their prostrations; two or three females, wrapped in their feredgés, stand near one of the doors, and a porter, with his head supported on the base of a pillar, is sleeping with all his might. A soft and tender light falls from the elevated windows; and I can see, in the distant recess, opposite the pulpit, the sparkle of the golden gratings of the tribune reserved for the Sultan.

A species of platform, supported by columns of finest marble and ornamented with carved railings, rises at each point of intersection of the aisles. In the side-chapels (useless in the Mussulman ritual), are heaped trunks, boxes, and packages of all kinds; for, in the East, the mosques serve as storehouses, and those who are going away on a journey, or who fear being robbed at home, deposit their wealth under the immediate protection of Allah; and there has never been an instance of the loss of a farthing under such circumstances, for theft would be also sacrilege. Heaps of dust accumulate upon masses of gold, or of precious objects, scarcely covered with wrappers of coarse cloth, or old leather; and the spider, so cherished among the Turks, for having thrown his web across the mouth of the cave in which the Prophet was concealed, weaves his thread peacefully about the locks, which no one takes the trouble to use.

Around the mosque are grouped hospitals, colleges, baths, and kitchens for the poor; for the whole of Moslem life gathers around the house of God. People without home sleep beneath the arches, where no police disturb them, for they are the guests of Allah. The faithful pray there; the females go there to dream away their time; and the sick are transported thither, to be cured or to die. In the East, the present life is never separated from religion and the thought of the future.

THÉOPHILE GAUTIER
Constantinople, 1853

The Innocents Abroad is a "record of a pleasure trip" undertaken in 1869 by America's beloved humorist and storyteller Samuel Langhorne Clemens — better known by his pen name, Mark Twain. Predictably, Constantinople repelled him and the much-touted Hagia Sophia left him distinctly unimpressed.

We dropped anchor in the mouth of the Golden Horn at daylight in the morning. Only three or four of us were up to see the great Ottoman capital. The passengers do not turn out at unseasonable hours, as they used to, to get the earliest possible glimpse of strange foreign cities. They are well over that. If we were lying in sight of the Pyramids of Egypt, they would not come on deck until after breakfast, now-a-days. . . .

. . . Seen from the anchorage or from a mile or so up the Bosporus, it is by far the handsomest city we have seen. Its dense array of houses swells upward from the water's edge, and spreads over the domes of many hills; and the gardens that peep out here and there, the great globes of the mosques, and the countless minarets that meet the eye every where, invest the metrop-

olis with the quaint Oriental aspect one dreams of when he reads books of eastern travel. Constantinople makes a noble picture.

But its attractiveness begins and ends with its picturesqueness. From the time one starts ashore till he gets back again, he execrates it. The boat he goes in is admirably miscalculated for the service it is built for. It is handsomely and neatly fitted up, but no man could handle it well in the turbulent currents that sweep down the Bosporus from the Black Sea, and few men could row it satisfactorily even in still water. It is a long, light canoe, (caique,) large at one end and tapering to a knife blade at the other. They make that long sharp end the bow, and you can imagine how these boiling currents spin it about. It has two oars, and sometimes four, and no rudder. You start to go to a given point and you run in fifty different directions before you get there. First one oar is backing water, and then the other; it is seldom that both are going ahead at once. This kind of boating is calculated to drive an impatient man mad in a week. The boatmen are the awkwardest, the stupidest, and the most unscientific on earth, without question.

Ashore, it was — well, it was an eternal circus. People were thicker than bees, in those narrow streets, and the men were dressed in all the outrageous, outlandish, idolatrous, extravagant, thunder-and-lightning costumes that ever a tailor with the delirium tremens and seven devils could conceive of. There was no freak in dress too crazy to be indulged in; no absurdity too absurd to be tolerated; no frenzy in ragged diabolism too fantastic to be attempted. No two men were dressed alike. It was a wild masquerade of all imaginable costumes — every struggling throng in every street was a dissolving view of stunning contrasts. Some patriarchs wore awful turbans, but the grand mass of the infidel horde wore the fiery red skull-cap they call a fez. All the remainder of the raiment they indulged in was utterly indescribable. . . .

The Mosque of St. Sophia is the chief lion of Constantinople. You must get a firman and hurry there the first thing. We did that. We did not get a firman, but we took along four or five francs apiece, which is much the same thing.

I do not think much of the Mosque of St. Sophia. I suppose I lack appreciation. We will let it go at that. It is the rustiest old barn in heathendom. I believe all the interest that attaches to it comes from the fact that it was built for a Christian church and then turned into a mosque, without much alteration, by the Mohammedan conquerors of the land. They made me take off my boots and walk into the place in my stocking-feet. I caught cold, and got myself so stuck up with a complication of gums, slime, and general corruption, that I wore out more than two thousand pair of boot-jacks getting my boots off that night, and even then some Christian hide peeled off with them. I abate not a single boot-jack.

St. Sophia is a colossal church, thirteen or fourteen hundred years old, and unsightly enough to be very, very much older. Its immense dome is said to be more wonderful than St. Peter's, but its dirt is much more wonderful than its dome, though they never mention it. The church has a hundred and seventy pillars in it, each a single piece, and all of costly marbles of various kinds, but they came from ancient temples at Baalbec, Heliopolis, Athens and Ephesus, and are battered, ugly and repulsive. They were a thousand years old when this church was new, and then the contrast must have been ghastly — if Justinian's architects did not trim them any. The inside of the dome is figured all over with a monstrous inscription in Turkish characters, wrought in gold mosaic, that looks as glaring as a circus bill; the pavements and the marble balustrades are all battered and dirty; the perspective is marred every where by a web of ropes that depend from the dizzy height of the dome, and suspend countless dingy, coarse oil lamps, and ostrich-eggs, six or seven feet above the floor. Squatting and sitting in groups, here and there and far and near, were ragged Turks reading books, hearing sermons, or receiving lessons like children, and in fifty places were more of the same sort bowing and straightening up, bowing again and getting down to kiss the earth, muttering prayers the while, and keeping up their gymnastics till they ought to have been tired, if they were not.

Every where was dirt, and dust, and dinginess, and gloom; every where were signs of a hoary antiquity, but with nothing touching or beautiful about it; every where were those groups of fantastic pagans; overhead the gaudy mosaics and the web of lamp-ropes — nowhere was there any thing to win one's love or challenge his admiration.

The people who go into ecstacies over St. Sophia must surely get them out of the guide-book (where every church is spoken of as being "considered by good judges to be the most marvelous structure, in many respects, that the world has ever seen.") Or else they are those old connoisseurs from the wilds of New Jersey who laboriously learn the difference between a fresco and a fire-plug and from that day forward feel privileged to void their critical bathos on painting, sculpture and architecture forever more.

SAMUEL LANGHORNE CLEMENS
The Innocents Abroad, 1869

In 1928, five years after the proclamation of the Turkish Republic, English novelist Arnold Bennett visited Constantinople. The author of The Old Wives' Tale, *a masterpiece of naturalistic prose, applied his acute powers of observation to the "new" Hagia Sophia.*

There is not a fez to be seen. Turkish costume has been abolished by ukase. Europe regarded the fez and the flowing robe as odd, quaint, typically Oriental, a sign of inferiority. Therefore these racial singularities had to be abolished. And they have been, completely. European costume is everywhere. I saw hardly a fez, except the rare white head-dress of priests. I saw only two or three veiled women, and hardly a yashmak [women's face veil]. But women move freely in the streets and the resorts. They prostrate themselves unveiled in mosques. They are, on the surface at any rate, totally enfranchised....

All is changed. (Not all, of course; by no means all, but much, and much of the kind that strikes the eye.) The changes sometimes are almost excruciating. See the interior of a mosque, where service is proceeding. Priests putting their foreheads to the ground in the Bagdad manner; the sparse congregation doing the same; a priest or muezzin high up somewhere in the church wailing his strange incantations. Yes; but the congregation wears cravats, neckties, overcoats; starched wristbands adorn the wrists.

Then there is the young Turkish Republic, intensely conscious of itself, eager, determined to assert itself. The fuss about passports on the ship, a fuss

that no magic of a laissez-passer could mitigate! One could have left an Atlantic liner in a third of the time. And the second fuss in the custom-house! And the third fuss over the police-forms in the hotel! . . .

Santa Sophia has been described continually for much more than a thousand years, and description of it must therefore be considered to be at an end. But I never knew, till I saw, that the entrance to it is in a charming garden, with an open-air café installed therein and flaneurs [men-about-town] smoking narghilehs [water pipes] which begin in a bubbling vessel and after travelling a few yards reach the mouths of the flaneurs (who *flanent* in silence, mysteriously).

It seems strange to me that the institution of slippers for infidels has survived into the new regime — especially as the slippers are much too large and every minute or so you are, without knowing it, leaving one of them behind you and desecrating the fane. Another strange thing (peculiar to this mosque) is that the minarets were added some ten centuries after the completion of the original structure, and yet, to my mind, harmonize with it. In Santa Sophia you can see characteristics which must have influenced Bentley when he was planning Westminster Cathedral.

The interior is tremendous. It will hold its own with anything in Europe. This dome has no air of being gigantic, yet is the largest in the world. Semi-domes cluster about it, and round these are small whole domes. The domes are like a family. The enormous floor is carpeted everywhere. The numerous chandeliers hang so low that they appear barely to escape your head; their chains rise aloft into invisibility. The general effect of the interior is blue and grey in the two tiers of arches, and above that broad gold with windows in heaven. The place is gloriously bare; all Christian symbols were removed when Santa Sophia changed over from Christ to Mahomet. All representations of the human figure have been either destroyed or covered with gold; but in one place you can distinguish beneath the gold the lineaments of Christ.

Nor have the Turks quite abandoned Christ. They take no chances. Within the lower part of a huge pillar is a carved image of Christ, and it is boxed up in stone and metal. But one little hole has been left. You can put your finger in this hole and touch the eye of the unseen image, in the hope of beneficent consequences.

Nobody can expect to behold a more grandiose, a finer, a more beautiful, a more logically designed, a more perfectly achieved, a more overwhelming temple than Santa Sophia. The legend sounds true enough that Justinian, entering it on its completion, remarked: "Solomon, I have surpassed thee."

Santa Sophia, however, is not Turkish; Turkish work upon it, done in obedience to religious sanctions, has been in no sense creative — rather destructive, though destructive with discretion.

Happily the prestige of the building was sufficient to prevent any such savage destruction as was wreaked upon most of the frescoes in the neglected Kahrieh Mosque, far away from the city wall. The frescoes which escaped the onslaught date from the thirteenth century, though you will be solemnly assured that they date from the fourth. They are very doubtfully said to be the earliest Christian frescoes surviving in a fair state of preservation; but beyond any question they are extremely beautiful and strange.

ARNOLD BENNETT
Mediterranean Scenes, 1928

In the late 1940's Herbert J. Muller assisted American architect Robert Van Nice
in the first comprehensive modern survey of Hagia Sophia. His book The Uses
of the Past *(Copyright 1952 by Oxford University Press, Inc.) pays special tribute*
to the humble artisans who built the monument.

I was working, a few years ago, in the cathedral of Hagia Sophia, in Istanbul.
Here was the great monument of Eastern Christendom. . . . From its famous
dome one might get a still longer and larger view of history, for it was completed by the Roman Emperor Justinian in the year 537 — six centuries
before Chartres — and it looks down on both Europe and Asia. And so I . . .
began to ponder the meanings of the past. Only, my reflections failed to produce a neat theory of history, or any simple, wholesome moral. Hagia Sophia,
or the 'Holy Wisdom,' gave me instead a fuller sense of the complexities,
ambiguities, and paradoxes of human history. . . .

At least I begin in simple piety. Although St. Sophia (as it is convention-
ally miscalled in the West) lacks the soaring grandeur of the Gothic cathedrals
and today is rather shabby in its ornateness — like an overdressed dowager
in decay — it remains a magnificent monument. It is not a degenerate form
of classic architecture but a daring creation in a new style; among other
things, its architects were the first to solve, on a large scale, the problem
of setting a spherical dome on a square chamber. Despite its ornateness
there is a majestic simplicity in its basic design, with the nave lined by
towering columns of porphyry and verd antique and crowned by the great
dome. One can still get a vivid idea of its original splendor, when the sunlight streaming in through the high windows of the dome made a glory
of the acres of gold-leaf mosaic on its vaulted ceilings — some four acres of
gold — and of the black, red, green, purple, and yellow marble of its paneled
walls. And St. Sophia would be impressive enough simply because it has
stood up for fourteen centuries, in constant use, withstanding hundreds
of earthquakes, surviving the rise and fall of empires — living out a longer
history than any other great building in Christendom.

Hence it is rich with the associations of all that has made Constantinople
so memorable in history. For nine hundred years St. Sophia was the main
stage for the high pageantry of the Byzantine Empire. Here presided the
Patriarchs of the Orthodox Church, the Bishops of Constantinople who
struggled with the Bishops of Rome and finally established their supremacy
in the East. Here the emperors were crowned and consecrated to the service
of the true faith, and here they gave thanks for their victories over the
enemies of Byzantium and God. In a real sense they owed their power to
St. Sophia, for the Orthodox Church was the chief unifying force of a hetero-
geneous empire. It was the Church that inspired the heroic resistance to the
all-conquering Arabs, which preserved Christendom in the East. Or it might
be called the power of the Virgin; for more than once, in popular belief,
it was only a miracle of the Virgin that saved Constantinople from conquest
by the heathens.

Yet simple piety is hardly the key to the history of this worldly city, or even
of St. Sophia. The Virgin no doubt had sufficient reason for allowing her
cathedral to fall to the Turks; in its subsequent history, at any rate, there
is an insistent irony of the crude Thomas Hardy type; and thereby hangs
my incongruous tale. Under the Ottoman Empire, Hagia Sophia served
as a mosque, resounding with praise of the very masculine Mohammed. A

few years ago this desecration was at last ended by Kemal Ataturk, the godless dictator who was himself attempting the miracle of creating a new Turkey on the Western model; he made the cathedral into a museum, in keeping with his policy of discouraging religion. An American architect was granted permission to make the first thorough study of the world-famous building. I relieved the architect of some routine work by making rubbings or copies of masons' marks — initials cut into the stones by the ancient builders. This simple task gave me the opportunity of crawling all over the stately monument, feeling my way back through the centuries, and working up a curious fond acquaintance with the anonymous masons. From these simple workmen I learned something more about the complexities of human history. . . .

From all appearances these artisans did not work in a holy, dedicated spirit. On some of the finer marble panels they left proud signatures, fancy monograms cut with loving care; but on most of the stones they chiseled out very crude initials. Apparently they made these marks in order to claim payment for their work; sometimes they signed a stone twice to make sure, with one signature upside down. I gathered that their primary motive was to get a job done and a living made, just as it is with workmen today. They differed from contemporary builders most obviously in that they did not work to exact specifications, but improvised as they went along. Their stones are generally rough-hewn, irregular in size or shape, and sometimes strangely imperfect. Instead of discarding, for example, a floor slab that had a broken corner or a crooked side, the masons cut the next one crooked so as to fit them together.

Upon close inspection, indeed, St. Sophia is an everlasting wonder in its anomalies. Its basic construction is honest, forthright, superbly solid; the more the architect learned about the secrets of its structure, the more he marveled at the resourcefulness and skill with which its builders had carried through an undertaking as bold and magnificent as the world had known, or yet knows. At the same time, there is hardly a straight line or a true curve in the majestic structure, even apart from the wear and tear of centuries. Everywhere one sees an exquisite care in the refinements of decoration, and an amateurish crudeness in the rudiments. The splendid columns of porphyry and verd antique are typical. Their capitals, and the arches resting on them, are elaborately carved; their bases are so roughly finished as to shame an apprentice. And in inconspicuous places even their ornamented capitals are likely to be unfinished. Everything stands; but everything is wavering, bulging, or askew.

The obvious excuse for such slovenliness in detail is the haste with which St. Sophia was erected; by a mighty effort, the Emperor Justinian succeeded in completing it in less than six years. This haste, however, suggests an unseemly impatience in his hopes of power in a future life. Justinian's piety is unquestionable — it is further proved by his savage persecution of heretics and his wars to extend the true faith. But it appears that he was also inspired by the hope of worldly fame that has led ordinary kings and capitalists to erect great monuments. . . . Carved all over St. Sophia is the monogram of Justinian and Theodora, the brilliant courtesan who became his empress. Outside the cathedral he set up a colossal equestrian statue of himself, as a modern Achilles. In his palace near by he required all officials to swear loyalty to "our divine and pious despots," Justinian and Theodora; all who entered the royal presence had to prostrate themselves and call themselves slaves. He maintained a personal sovereignty more absolute than any emperor before him. . . .

The succeeding generations of worshipers in St. Sophia left humbler tokens of their own aspirations to immortality. Scratched on the columns and balustrades in the galleries, where the women sat, are many ancient initials and doodlings, including satirical drawings of bishops in their ceremonial robes. On the main floor the piety was purer, though of a superstitious kind. Hollows worn in the pavement beside the columns indicate where countless worshipers stood to kiss the holy icons; a hole in the "perspiring column" of St. Gregory betokens the faith of countless more, who rubbed their fingers here to cure or prevent eye trouble. But less edifying are the memorials of royal worshipers. Among the superb mosaics, for instance, is a portrait of the Empress Zoe, who ascended the throne as a middle-aged virgin and devoted herself chiefly to making amends for her prolonged chastity. Beside her is her husband Constantine Monomachos, who looks somewhat strange because his head is set on shoulders belonging to somebody else; he had been preceded by two husbands who turned out badly. . . .

What, then, does St. Sophia have to tell us? . . . St. Sophia remains an inspiring monument, glorious and vainglorious. It is a symbol of humility and pride, of holiness and worldliness, of the power of faith and the limitations of faith. It is an everlasting triumph, of a society that failed. It may epitomize all the great societies and golden ages of the past, which also failed and still inspire.

HERBERT J. MULLER
The Uses of the Past, 1952

REFERENCE

Chronology

1205–16	Reign of Henry I, ablest of Latin emperors
1228–61	Reign of Baldwin II, last Latin emperor
1261	Greeks recapture Constantinople and restore Byzantine Empire; **Michael VIII, founder of the Palaeologi, crowned emperor in Hagia Sophia**
1317	**Andronicus II adds pyramidal tower-buttresses**
1344	**Serious earthquake damages Hagia Sophia**
1346	**Eastern arch collapses**
1346–56	**Major restoration undertaken**
1391	**Coronation of Manuel II Palaeologus in Hagia Sophia**
1397	Abortive siege of Constantinople by Turks
1422	Second Ottoman siege fails to capture city of Constantinople
1439	Council of Florence proposes Act of Union between Roman and Orthodox churches
1448–53	Reign of Constantine XI, last of the Byzantine emperors
1452	**Act of Union with Rome celebrated in Hagia Sophia**
1453	Fall of Constantinople to Ottoman Sultan Mohammed II — following brutal seven-week siege of city — brings an end to Christian Constantinople; **Hagia Sophia converted into a mosque and consecrated to Moslem worship**
1481	Death of Mohammed the Conqueror
1520–66	Expansion of Ottoman Empire during reign of Suleiman the Magnificent
1566–74	**Reign of Selim II, who adds a minaret to the northwest corner of the mosque**
1571	Turks suffer major defeat at battle of Lepanto
1573	**Sinan adds new supporting buttresses to Hagia Sophia**
1574–95	**Reign of Murad III, who adds two more minarets**
1623–40	**Reign of Murad IV, who commissions railed balconies for interior of mosque**
1683	Ottoman forces fail to take Vienna
1703–30	**Reign of Ahmed III, builder of a new sultan's box**
c. **1750**	**Interior mosaics obscured with whitewash**
1766	**Earthquakes damage Hagia Sophia**
1821–31	Greek war of independence
1826	Destruction of the Janissaries
1847	**Full restoration of Hagia Sophia begun by Swiss architects Gaspare and Giuseppe Fossati during reign of Abdul Medjid**
1849	**Restored Hagia Sophia inaugurated**
1853–56	Crimean War with Russia
1876	Proclamation of first Turkish constitution following deposition of Sultan Abdul-Aziz; accession of Abdul-Hamid II
1894	**Earthquake damages interior decoration**
1908	Revolution of the Young Turks; temporary restoration of Constitution of 1876
1909	Abdul-Hamid II, last absolute ruler, deposed and succeeded by his brother Mohammed V
1912–13	Turkey loses most of its European territory as a result of the Balkan Wars
1913	Coup d'etat of the Young Turks
1914	Turkey enters World War I on the side of the Central Powers
1918	Collapse of Turkish armies; Allies occupy and rule Istanbul
1918–22	Reign of Mohammed VI, last Ottoman sultan
1919	Mustafa Kemal organizes national resistance movement to prevent dismemberment of the Turkish nation
1922	Abolition of the sultanate
1923	Treaty of Lausanne between Allies and Turkey; proclamation of a Turkish Republic; election of Mustafa Kemal as president; Angora renamed Ankara and declared capital of Turkey
1923–38	Westernization of Turkey; Islam no longer the state religion
1930	Constantinople officially renamed Istanbul
1932	**Work begun on restoration of mosaics**
1934	**Hagia Sophia reopened as a secular museum**
1935	Mustafa Kemal adopts name of Atatürk
1938	Death of Atatürk
1939–45	Turkey maintains nonbelligerent status during World War II
1950	Turkey joins NATO
1967	**Pope Paul pays official visit to Hagia Sophia**

Guide to the Mosques of Istanbul

The long and illustrious history of Hagia Sophia as a Christian church came to an abrupt and cataclysmic end in 1453. In May of that year Sultan Mohammed II conquered Constantinople and consecrated the basilica to Moslem worship.

During the next two hundred years Hagia Sophia served as a model and inspiration for the extraordinary building fervor of Ottoman sultans, members of the ruling family, government officials, and wealthy individuals. Many former churches were converted into mosques; many more new structures were designed specifically as temples of Islam. Utilizing the basic form of a domed structure, which they adopted from Hagia Sophia, the Turks totally transformed the physical appearance of their new capital. In the process, they created a viable and innovative architectural style suited to the Moslem faith.

The Moslem mode of prayer dictated that the mosque be a single open forum, with no area more sacred than any other. Since the Prophet had forbidden the representation of human and animal forms, the Turks mastered the art of abstract ornamentation. A profusion of superlative geometric, floral, and calligraphic designs adorns the interiors of their mosques. A sense of structural grandeur and spaciousness, combined with a minute attention to decorative detail, epitomizes Ottoman architecture at its best.

The first imperial mosque built in Constantinople (unofficially renamed Istanbul by the Turks) was the *Mosque of the Conqueror,* known as the *Fatih.* Mohammed II engaged the services of a Greek convert to Islam, the architect

Christodoulos. In 1463 Christodoulos began work on the city's fourth hill, on the site of the ruins of the Church of the Holy Apostles — which had been rebuilt by Justinian in the sixth century and had served as the burial place for the Byzantine emperors.

The Fatih, completed in 1471, consisted of a vast domed edifice buttressed by a single half dome. Nothing remains of Mohammed's mosque today, for it was completely destroyed by a violent earthquake in 1677. For almost a century the mosque lay in ruins before Sultan Mustafa III decided to rebuild it. The new mosque, designed by Sarim Ibrahim Pasa in a semi-Italian style with four half domes supporting a large central dome, was reopened in 1771. The structure is noted more for its immense size than for the originality of its plan.

Within the mosque is an Arabic inscription that recalls the Conqueror's prophecy: "Constantinople will fall; happy the army that shall conquer her and glorious its leader." To the southeast of the mosque complex is the *turbeh,* or tomb, of Mohammed II, which dates from 1782. Its interior is richly carved and decorated; the sultan's remains lie under an elaborate catafalque topped by a huge turban.

The *Mosque of Beyazid II,* built between 1501 and 1506 by the architect Haydreddin, was the first to be directly inspired by the ground plan of Hagia Sophia. It set the pattern for the monumental imperial mosques of the six-

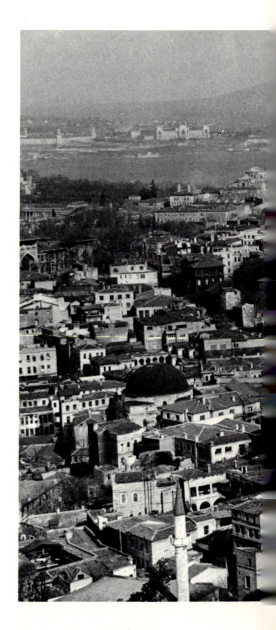

The striking skyline of modern Istanbul (right) presents a mélange of small private dwellings and large imperial mosques.

teenth and seventeenth centuries.

Leading to the mosque is a square courtyard with columned porticoes — the first of its kind. The columns, of granite and jasper, support pointed arches — and each of the twenty-four bays formed by the arches is topped by a small dome. In the center of the courtyard is the ritual ablutions fountain — a feature common to all Moslem mosques — where the faithful wash before entering.

Hundreds of pigeons swarm about the courtyard — and the building is popularly known as the Pigeons' Mosque. According to legend, Beyazid II purchased the first pair of birds from a poor widow and donated them to the mosque.

Upon entering the mosque from the courtyard, one encounters a long corridor resembling the narthex of Byzantine churches, whose wings extend beyond the square nave. The cupola or dome rests on four triangular sections of vaulting known as pendentives. Windows cut into the dome shed luminous light on the interior. As in all mosques there are no pews or chairs; worshipers stand or kneel on the floor, which is covered with carpets in the winter and mats in the summer.

Unlike the original Fatih, the Pigeons' Mosque has two half domes to the east and west of the central one. Other smaller domes complete the roofing. Less than half the size of Hagia Sophia, the nave interior forms one unbroken mass flanked by two wide aisles. There are no upper galleries, only a small balcony over the entrance.

The direction of Mecca — the *qibla* — determines the positioning of all Moslem mosques. Set into the *qibla* wall is the *mihrab*, or niche, which is the focal point for prayer. In the Pigeons' Mosque the *mihrab* is decorated with stalactites, tiers of small pointed arches.

A feature of most Moslem mosques is the minaret, or tower from which the faithful are called to prayer five times a day by the *muezzins*, or criers. Two pointed minarets form part of the Mosque of Beyazid II and add sharp vertical lines to the graceful arcs of the soaring domes.

Among the many mosques erected in Istanbul by Suleiman the Magnificent is one dedicated to his father. The outstanding feature of the *Mosque of Selim I*, which was built between 1520 and 1522, is the decoration of the rectangular courtyard. Eighteen columns with stalactite capitals support twenty-two cupolas; below the domes are particularly lovely lunettes and faience work.

The plan of the mosque itself is unusual: a large dome is supported by four immense pendentives. Extensions to the north and south each consist of chambers roofed by nine smaller domes. The *mihrab* and the *minbar*, a box or pulpit used for special occasions, are of fine marquetry. The overall effect of the interior is one of austerity and simplicity.

The *Sehzade*, completed in 1548, was the first mosque built in Istanbul by Sinan, the most talented of all Turkish architects. A Janissary who had served as a military engineer, he was appointed chief architect to Sultan Suleiman the Magnificent. Between the ages of fifty and eighty-nine, Sinan erected 131 mosques as well as several hundred other structures throughout the Ottoman Empire. Almost singlehandedly Sinan created the golden age of Turkish imperial architecture.

As a result of a court intrigue inspired by his wife Roxelana — who spread false rumors about the perfidy of Suleiman's eldest son, Prince Mustafa, in order to advance the cause of her own son, Selim — the sultan himself strangled the prince. Regretting the murder, Suleiman had the Sehzade built in Mustafa's memory.

The Sehzade has a lovely three-gated courtyard. Its sixteen cupolas are supported by twelve marble and granite columns surmounted by distinctly Ottoman stalactite capitals. Each of the two polygonal minarets at the eastern end is decorated with carved geometrical motifs.

The Mosque of Beyazid II, which had been built by Sinan's teacher, has only two half domes. In the Sehzade, Sinan improved on that design and created greater symmetry by adding two additional half domes at the north and south. At the corners are four smaller cupolas. The main dome, which is supported by four octagonal pillars, is pierced by twenty-four large stained-glass windows.

Built for his imperial patron between 1550 and 1557, the *Mosque of Suleiman the Magnificent* — known as the *Suleimaniye* — is considered one of the masterpieces of Sinan's career. Upon completing the majestic gray stone structure, Sinan is reputed to have said: "I have built for thee, O Emperor, a mosque that will remain on the face of the earth till the day of judgment." The largest and most sumptuous mosque in Istanbul, the Suleimaniye is surrounded by a complex of other buildings that were originally used as schools, hospitals, and a home for the poor. To the east are the *turbehs* of Suleiman and Roxelana.

The mosque is reached by a porticoed

rectangular courtyard that is paved in white marble. Eighteen elegant cupolas rest on twenty-four monolithic columns that were originally part of the Byzantine Hippodrome. The rectangular ablutions fountain is adorned with bronze grillwork and marble reliefs. Five doors lead directly into the mosque.

At the corners of the courtyard are four sharply pointed minarets which symbolize the fact that Suleiman was the fourth sultan since the conquest of the city. And their total of ten balconies indicates that he was the tenth sultan since the founding of the dynasty.

Resting on four huge piers and supported by numerous semidomes, the rectangular Suleimaniye has a central dome that is higher in proportion but smaller in span than that of Hagia Sophia. Sinan had hoped to surpass the church's measurements as well, but he did not succeed in doing so until the end of his career, when he designed the Selim Mosque in Adrianople (modern Edirne).

The Suleimaniye relies for its impact largely on its overwhelming proportions and on the light that floods the interior from its windowed tympana, a device borrowed from Hagia Sophia. (In all, 138 stained-glass windows illuminate the interior.) Otherwise there is little true affinity of character or purpose between the two structures.

Hagia Sophia is essentially a basilica, with parallel colonnades and aisles matched by galleries above. The Suleimaniye is an open hall of prayer, radially planned beneath its dome, without nave or sanctuary and with open, broadly arcaded side aisles roofed by five unequal cupolas. It is a shrine free from mystery or concealment, since all parts of it are visible at once.

In its sublime conception of space, the interior of Hagia Sophia far outshines Suleiman's mosque. The light, ordered symmetry of the mosque's exterior, on the other hand, far outclasses the confused, ponderous exterior of the church. The skillful and logical groupings of the half domes and lesser domes of the Suleimaniye rise in rhythmical stages to the great dome with an easy assurance that Hagia Sophia, condemned through its history to a series of improvisations, never achieved.

To the east of the former Byzantine Hippodrome and on the site of the royal palaces is the *Mosque of Ahmed I.* It was built between 1609 and 1617 by the architect Daoud, a pupil of Sinan. In the nineteenth century, it was the departure point for caravans of pilgrims setting out for Mecca.

Considered one of the most beautiful mosques in the city and a leading tourist attraction, it is known as the Blue Mosque in tribute to the incomparable enameled blue and white faience tiles that line the interior to the height of the upper windows. The mosque is surrounded on three sides by a vast, walled courtyard entered through five monumental bronze gates. The rectangular marble forecourt that leads to the mosque is lined with twenty-six granite columns — topped by marble stalactite capitals — that support thirty cupolas. The small hexagonal fountain made of marble is richly decorated with elaborate floral designs.

The mosque has six well-proportioned minarets. To atone for his arrogance in equaling the number of minarets at the mosque in Mecca, Ahmed I had a seventh added to the holy city's shrine.

Within the rectangular mosque, the huge dome is supported by four fluted circular piers, known as "elephant's feet" because of their massiveness. Surrounding the central dome are four large half domes and four smaller full domes. The 260 windows that illuminate the interior were once filled with stained glass; today harsh sunlight streams through the clear glass panes.

The *Yeni Valide,* or *New Mosque,* was the last of the great imperial mosques constructed during the golden age of the Ottoman Empire. It was begun in 1598 by the architect Daoud for Sultana Safiye, mother of Mohammed III, but work was halted upon the sultan's death in 1603. The mosque was finally completed in 1663 by Mustafa Aga with funds provided by the mother of Mohammed IV.

The ornate octagonal ablutions fountain in the center of the porticoed courtyard is a treasure of Turkish art. Semicolumns, stalactite decoration, sculpture, and grillwork create a harmonious whole. Two minarets, each with three galleries, appear at the sides of the broad courtyard.

The interior of the Yeni Valide is similar in plan to the Sehzade and Ahmed mosques. Laid out on a rectangular plan, the central dome is upheld by four pointed arches that rest on four pendentives. Each of four large semidomes is flanked by two smaller semidomes. Beautiful floral and geometric motifs adorn the interior. Both the *mihrab* and *minbar* are ornamented with sculpture and gilding. Wide colonnaded galleries form sweeping aisles that add to the grace of the mosque.

Selected Bibliography

Beckwith, Jean. *The Art of Constantinople*. London: Phaidon Press Ltd., 1968.

Creasy, Edward S. *History of the Ottoman Turks*. Beirut: Khayats, 1961.

Grabar, André. *Byzantine Painting*. New York: Skira, 1953.

Hitti, Philip K. *History of the Arabs*. New York: St. Martin's Press, Inc., 1961.

Hutter, Irmgard. *Early Christian and Byzantine Art*. New York: Universe Books, 1971.

Kahler, Heinz. *Hagia Sophia*. New York: Frederick A. Praeger, Publishers, 1967.

Kinross, Lord. *Atatürk: The Rebirth of a Nation*. New York: William Morrow and Company, 1965.

————. *Turkey*. New York: The Viking Press, 1959.

————. *Within the Taurus: A Journey in Asiatic Turkey*. New York: William Morrow and Company, 1955.

Lassus, Jean. *The Early Christian and Byzantine World*. London: Paul Homlyn, 1967.

Lewis, Bernard. *Istanbul and the Civilization of the Ottoman Empire*. Norman, Okla.: University of Oklahoma Press, 1963.

Mango, Cyril. *The Mosaics of St. Sophia at Istanbul*. Washington, D.C.: The Dumbarton Oaks Research and Library Collection, 1962.

Ramsaur, Ernest Edmondson, Jr. *The Young Turks*. Princeton: Princeton University Press, 1957.

Rice, David Talbot. *The Art of Byzantium*. New York: Harry N. Abrams, Inc., 1959.

Runciman, Steven. *Byzantine Civilisation*. London: Edward Arnold Ltd., 1933.

Sherrard, Philip. *Constantinople, Iconography of a Sacred City*. London: Oxford University Press, 1965.

Swift, Emerson Howland. *Hagia Sofia*. New York: Columbia University Press, 1940.

Ünsal, Behçet. *Turkish Islamic Architecture in Seljuk and Ottoman Times*. New York: Transatlantic Arts, Inc., 1970.

Vryonis, Speros, Jr. *Byzantium and Europe*. London: Thames and Hudson, 1967.

Acknowledgments and Picture Credits

The Editors make grateful acknowledgment for the use of excerpted material from the following works:

A History of the Crusades by Steven Runciman. Copyright 1951 by Steven Runciman. The excerpt appearing on page 73 is reproduced by permission of Mr. Runciman and Cambridge University Press.

Hagia Sophia by Heinz Kahler. Translated by Ellyn Childs. Copyright 1967 by Gebrueder Mann Verlag GMBH. The excerpt appearing on page 102 is reproduced by permission of Praeger Publishers and Gebrueder Mann Verlag GMBH.

Mediterranean Scenes by Arnold Bennett. Copyright 1928 by Arnold Bennett. The excerpt appearing on pages 156–57 is reproduced by permission of Mrs. Dorothy Cheston Bennett.

My Russian and Turkish Journals by Lady Hariot Dufferin. Copyright 1916 by Lady Hariot Dufferin. The excerpt appearing on page 151 is reproduced by permission of John Murray Ltd.

On Buildings by Procopius. Translated by B. H. Dewing and Glanville Downey. Copyright 1940 by Loeb Classical Library. The excerpts appearing on pages 14, 138–40 are reproduced by permission of Harvard University Press and the Loeb Classical Library.

The Church of Sancta Sophia by William R. Lethaby and Harold Swainson. Copyright 1894 by Macmillan & Co. Ltd. The excerpt appearing on page 14 is reproduced by permission of Macmillan & Co. Ltd.

The Conquest of Constantinople by Robert of Clari. Translated by Edgar Holmes McNeal. Copyright 1936 by Columbia University Press. The excerpt appearing on page 142 is reproduced by permission of Columbia University Press.

Travels and Adventures of Pero Tafur. Translated and edited by Malcolm Letts. Copyright 1926 by Routledge & Kegan Paul Ltd. The excerpt appearing on page 144 is reproduced by permission of Routledge & Kegan Paul Ltd.

The Travels of Ibn Battuta. Translated by C. Defremery and B. R. Sanguinetti. Copyright 1962 by Cambridge University Press for the Hakluyt Society. The excerpt appearing on page 142 is reproduced by permission of Cambridge University Press.

The Uses of the Past by Herbert J. Muller. Copyright 1952 by Oxford University Press. The excerpt appearing on pages 158–60 is reproduced by permission of Oxford University Press.

The Editors would like to express their particular appreciation to Professor Cyril Mango of the Center for Byzantine Studies, Dumbarton Oaks, Washington, D.C., for his critical comments on the text, and to Ara Guler in Istanbul for his creative photography. In addition, the Editors would like to thank the following organizations and individuals:

Jane de Cabanyes, Madrid
Marilyn Flaig, Susan Storer, New York
Lydia Hancock, Rome
Kate Lewin, Paris

Dumbarton Oaks — Caroline Backlund,
    Susan Boyd, Judith O'Neill
New York University, Institute of Fine Arts —
    Harry Bober

The title or description of each picture appears after the page number (boldface), followed by its location. Photographic credits appear in parentheses. The following abbreviations are used:

BV,R — Biblioteca Vaticana, Rome
BN,P — Bibliothèque Nationale, Paris
(DO) — Courtesy of Dumbarton Oaks, Washington, D.C.
TPM,I (AG) — Topkapi Palace Museum, Istanbul (Ara Guler)
TSM,V (MP) — Treasury of St. Mark's, Venice (Mauro Pucciarelli)

ENDPAPERS Vault mosaic in narthex of Hagia Sophia (DO) HALF TITLE Symbol designed by Jay J. Smith Studio FRONTISPIECE Incense burner in the shape of a Byzantine church, 12th century. TSM,V (MP) **9** Chalice taken from Constantinople after the sack of 1204. TSM,V (MP) **10-11** Interior of Hagia Sophia (Ara Guler) **12-13** Miniature of worshipers in Hagia Sophia, from *Skylitzes Chronicle*, 13th century. Biblioteca Nacional, Madrid (Oronoz) fol 115v

CHAPTER I **15** Byzantine ivory of the Empress Ariadne, *c.* 500. Museo Nazionale, Florence (Alinari) **16** Detail from miniature of Constantine I on the Milvian Bridge, from *The Homilies of Gregory of Nazianzus, c.* 880. BN,P, Ms. Grec. 510 **17** Map by Francis & Shaw, Inc. **18** Cameo of Constantine I and his family. Stadtbibliothek, Trier **19** Bronze head of Constantine I. Museo dei Conservatori, Rome (Josephine Powell) **20** Two bronze pagan-Christian patens, 4th century. Campo Santo Teutonico, Rome **21** Ivory carving of family watching games in the Hippodrome in Constantinople, from the Diptych of Lampadii, *c.* 355. Museo Cristiano, Brescia (Mauro Pucciarelli) **22** Miniature of the Council of Constantinople in 381, from *The Homilies of Gregory of Nazianzus, c.* 880. BN,P, Ms. Grec. 510, fol 355 **23** top, Miniature of Gregory and Theodosius after the council of 381; bottom, Miniature of Orthodox Christians fleeing the Arians. Both from *The Homilies of Gregory of Nazianzus, c.* 880. BN,P, Ms. Grec. 510, fols 239 & 367v **25** Miniature of St. John Chrysostom presenting the Emperor Nicephorus III Botaniates with his sermons, from *The Homilies of St. John Chrysostom*, 11th century. BN,P, Ms. Coislin 79, fol 2v **26** Byzantine ivory with personification of Constantinople, 5th century. Kunsthistorisches Museum, Vienna **27** Reverse of a coin commemorating the founding of Constantinople, *c.* 330. Civico Medagliere Milanese, Milan **28-29** Aerial photograph of Hagia Sophia (Ara Guler)

CHAPTER II **31** Byzantine ivory diptych belonging to Justinian, *c.* 521. Castello Sforzesco, Milan (Mario Perotti) **32** Miniature of Justinian ordering the building of Hagia Sophia, from the *Chronicle of Manasses.* BV,R, Codex Vaticanus Slavonicus 2, fol 109r **34** Interior of the dome of Hagia Sophia (Ara Guler) **35** Exterior of the dome of Hagia Sophia (Josephine Powell) **36-37** The columns at Hagia Sophia (Ara Guler) **38, 39** Capital of a column at Hagia Sophia; Interior view of Hagia Sophia. Both (Ara Guler) **40** Silver gilt cross of Justin II, 565-78. Treasury of St. Peter's, Vatican (Mauro Pucciarelli) **42, 43** Imperial doors of Hagia Sophia; Detail of the relief over the imperial doors of Hagia Sophia. Both (DO) **44** Miniature of the construction of Solomon's temple, Constantinople, 4th century. BN,P, Ms. Grec. 20 fol 4r

CHAPTER III **47** Byzantine ivory casket, 9th-10th century. Metropolitan Museum of Art, Gift of J. Pierpont Morgan, 1917 **48** Miniature of the Ascension of Christ, from a book of sermons by the monk Jacob of Kokkinobaphos, 12th century. BV,R, Ms. Grec. 1162 fol 2v **50** Obverse and reverse of a medallion of Justinian, 534-38. British Museum (John Webb) **51** top, Mosaic of Justinian and his court; bottom, Mosaic of Theodora and her court: Both, *c.* 547. Church of San Vitale, Ravenna (Mauro Pucciarelli) **53** The Barberini Ivory of Justinian, *c.* 527. Louvre **54, 55** Nave of Hagia Sophia seen through the main door of the narthex; Detail from mosaic of Christ and the archangel Gabriel above the main door of the narthex. Both (Ara Guler) **56** Miniature of the Iconoclasts whitewashing an image of Christ from a psalter made in Constantinople, 1066. British Museum, Ms. Add. 19352 fol 27v **57** Mosaic framed window in the apse of Hagia Sophia (DO) **58** Mosaic of Justinian, the Virgin and Child, and Constantine over the south door of Hagia Sophia, 986-94 (Ara Guler) **59** Detail of the mosaic showing Justinian offering Hagia Sophia to the Virgin, 986-94 (DO) **60** Mosaic of the Virgin and Child in the bema at Hagia Sophia, 9th century (DO) **61** top, Detail of the mosaic of the archangel Gabriel in the bema at Hagia Sophia, 9th century (DO); bottom, Mosaic of Christ Pantocrator between Constantine IX Monomachus and Zoë in the south gallery at Hagia Sophia, 1028-42 (Ara Guler) **62** Colonnades and arches at Hagia Sophia (Ara Guler) **64** left, Mosaic detail of the Virgin Mary; right, Mosaic detail of St. John the Baptist **65** Mosaic detail of Christ. All from the mosaic of the Deesis in the south gallery of Hagia Sophia, 13th century (Ara Guler)

CHAPTER IV **67** Byzantine ivory casket lid showing the capture of a walled city, 11th century. The Cathedral Treasury, Troyes (Giraudon) **68** top, Miniature of the conquest of Edessa, 1098; bottom, Miniature of the defense of Constantinople, 1046. Both from the *Skylitzes Chronicle*, 13th century.

Biblioteca Nacional, Madrid (Oronoz) fols 205 & 230v **69** Miniature of Alexius I Comnenus and Christ. BV,R, Ms. Grec. 666, fol 2v **70** Miniature of a Crusader at prayer, from *Chronicles* by Matthew Paris. British Museum, Ms. Roy. 2.A.xxii. fol 220 **72** Miniature of the conquest of Constantinople, 1204, from *Chronicles of the Crusades,* by Count Geoffroy de Villehardouin, 13th century. Bodleian Library, Oxford, Ms. Laud. Misc. 587 fol 1 **74** top, Back of the silver gilt and enamel Beresford Hope Cross, 9th century. Victoria and Albert Museum, London; bottom, Gold and enamel book cover with the archangel Michael, 10th century. TSM,V (MP) **75** top, Alabaster paten with center enamel of Christ, 11th century; bottom, Sardonyx and silver gilt chalice, 12th century. TSM,V (MP) **77** Byzantine ivory chair of Maximian, *c.* 545. Archiepiscopal Museum, Ravenna (Anderson) **78, 79** Outer and inner reliquaries for the True Cross, *c.* 960. Cathedral Treasury, Limburg an der Lahn **80** Bronze horses at St. Mark's Cathedral, Venice (Alinari) **83** Miniature of the coronation of Baldwin of Flanders in Hagia Sophia, from *Histoire de Jerusalem,* 13th century. BN,P, Ms. Fr. 9081, fol 99v

CHAPTER V **85** Byzantine ivory of the crowning of Constantine VII Porphyrogenitus, *c.* 944. Museum of Fine Arts, Moscow (Hirmer Verlag) **86** top, Obverse of a medallion of Emperor John VIII Palaeologus by Antonio Pisanello, 15th century. British Museum (John Webb); bottom, Emperor John VIII Palaeologus, detail from *The Procession of the Magi,* by Benozzo Gozzoli, 1459. Palazzo Riccardi, Florence (Mauro Pucciarelli) **87** Emperor John VIII Palaeologus, detail from the bronze doors at St. Peter's, Rome, by Filarete, 1445 (Anderson) **89** Portrait of Sultan Mohammed II by Gentile Bellini, 1480. TPM,I (AG) **90** Sketch of a Janissary by Gentile Bellini, 1480. British Museum, Ms. Roy. 4. P.&P. 7 **92** Miniature of Constantinople and the Bosporus, from *Liber Insularum Archipelagi,* by Buondelmonte, 1420. BN,P **93** Turkish miniature of princes guarded by pages and Janissaries, 16th century. TPM,I (AG) **94-95** Constantinople's land walls (Ara Guler) **97** Miniature of the siege of Constantinople in 1453, from *Passages d'Outremer* by Jean Mielot, 15th century. BN,P, Ms. Fr. 9087, fol 207v **98** The gravestones of Ottoman soldiers outside the walls of Constantinople (Ara Guler) **100** Miniature of the Conqueror, Sultan Mohammed, beside the Serpentine Column in Constantinople's Hippodrome, 16th century. TPM,I (AG) **101** The "Epitaphios Sindon" shroud, *c.* 1407. Victoria and Albert Museum, London (John Webb)

CHAPTER VI **103** One of three sections of a Byzantine-Venetian ivory book cover, 13th century. Victoria and Albert Museum, London **104** Portrait of Sultan Mohammed the Conqueror by Sinan Bey, 16th century. TPM,I (AG) **105** Bronze central door to the narthex at Hagia Sophia (DO) **106, 107** left, Engraving of Hagia Sophia; right, Engraving of the Suleimaniye. Both from *Relation Nouvelle d'un Voyage de Constantinople,* by Guillaume Joseph Grelot, Paris, 1680 (DO) **108** Calligraphic signature of Suleiman the Magnificent. TPM,I (AG) **109** Portrait of Suleiman the Magnificent and attendants by Nigari, 16th century. TPM,I (AG) **110** Drawing of the interior of Hagia Sophia by Cornelius Loos, 1710. National Museum, Stockholm (DO) **110-111** Two architectural drawings of Hagia Sophia by Charles Texier, 1834. Royal Institute of British Architects (DO) **112** Engraving of the nave of Hagia Sophia, from *Aya Sofia* by Chevalier Fossati, London, 1852 (DO) **114-15** Engraving of the exterior of Hagia Sophia, from *Aya Sofia* by Chevalier Fossati, London, 1852 (DO) **117** Engraving of the nave of Hagia Sophia, from *Aya Sofia,* by Chevalier Fossati, London, 1852 (DO) **118** The sultan's box in Hagia Sophia (DO) **121** Interior of Hagia Sophia with an alabaster vase in foreground (Ara Guler)

CHAPTER VII **123** One of three sections of a Byzantine-Venetian ivory book cover, 13th century. Victoria and Albert Museum, London **124-25** Sunset at Hagia Sophia (Ara Guler) **127** Mustafa Kemal (Brown Brothers) **128** Mosaic of Justinian, the Virgin and Child, and Constantine over the south door of Hagia Sophia, 986-94 (Ara Guler) **129** both, The progressive uncovering of the mosaic (DO) **130** Ernest Hawkins, Edwin Angst, and John Brennan working on mosaics of saints John Chrysostom and Ignatius Theophorus in the north tympanum of Hagia Sophia (DO) **131** The mosaic of St. John Chrysostom uncovered in the north tympanum of Hagia Sophia, 10th century (DO) **132** Iron cramp installed on mosaics by the Fossati brothers, *c.* 1849 (DO) **133** Mosaic of the Emperor Alexander in the north gallery of Hagia Sophia, 10th century (DO) **134** Porphyry dolphins on the west wall of the nave at Hagia Sophia (DO) **135** Mosaic of the archangel Gabriel in the bema of Hagia Sophia, 9th century (DO)

HAGIA SOPHIA IN LITERATURE **136** Architectural plan of the cupolas of Hagia Sophia by Charles Texier, 1834. Royal Institute of British Architects (DO) **138-39** Fountain and square of Hagia Sophia **140-41** Interior of the Suleimaniye mosque **144-45** Coffee kiosque on the port **146-47** Suleimaniye from the Seraskier's Tower **150-51** A public khan **154-55** Interior of Hagia Sophia **156-57** The Burnt Pillar **160** The floating bridge. Lithographs on pages 138-60 by W. H. Bartlett, from *The Beauties of the Bosphorus* by Miss Pardoe, London, 1838 (DO)

REFERENCE **164-65** Aerial photograph of Istanbul (Ara Guler)

Index